To Love and to Cherish

The Pastor's Manual
for Premarital Counseling
in The United Methodist Church

The Methodist Publishing House, Nashville, Tennessee

TO LOVE AND TO CHERISH

Copyright © 1970 by The Methodist Publishing House

ISBN 0-687-42248-5

SET UP, PRINTED, AND BOUND BY THE
PARTHENON PRESS, AT NASHVILLE,
TENNESSEE, UNITED STATES OF AMERICA

Foreword

The Book of Discipline places upon all United Methodist churches and pastors the responsibility of Christian education for marriage, parenthood, and family living. It specifically directs pastors to counsel with couples planning to be married. "He shall hold premarital conferences, using the official manual of the Church" (Paragraph 350. 5a).

The 1956 General Conference of The Methodist Church approved and referred to the General Board of Education for implementation a memorial that reads in part as follows:

WHEREAS . . . an official marriage manual for use by couples contemplating marriage would greatly strengthen and support the pastor's efforts to provide better preparation for marriage,

NOW, THEREFORE BE IT RESOLVED that such an official manual be prepared. . .

Accordingly the Board of Education called a consultation including pastors and others doing premarital counseling, professors of pastoral care in our seminaries, youth, adult, and student work specialists, and staff members of the Board of Education with special responsibility for Christian family life education.

The Curriculum Committee of The Methodist Church approved descriptions of a manual for couples and one for pastors, and a panel of consultants was chosen to give guidance throughout the process of developing the manuals. In due time the manuals were produced and widely used.

In this tradition the Program-Curriculum Committee of The United Methodist Church again approved descriptions for marriage manuals on December 3, 1968. Writers were set to work, a panel of consultants was chosen, and pastors in selected local churches were invited to give guidance throughout the process of developing the manuals.

The writers, who remain anonymous because the manuals are the product of many minds and will serve as official manuals for the entire church, have performed a most important service for the church. To them, to the consultants, and to all others who have assisted in producing the marriage manuals of The United Methodist Church, let me express appreciation on behalf of the Board of Education.

As the pastor studies this book, he should also familiarize himself with the contents of the couples' manual entitled *To Love and to Cherish*. He should have enough copies on hand to present one to each couple coming to set the date for their marriage. Administrative boards will doubtless want the church treasury to provide *To Love and to Cherish* just as it provides the membership manuals for the pastor's classes. With the information contained in these two books and in the questionnaires in the couples' manual, which the couple fill out, we hope the pastor will feel better prepared for the counseling sessions.

4

We trust that these official manuals of the church, prepared with the hearty cooperation of so many competent people, will prove a blessing to thousands of couples as they enter holy matrimony.

Henry M. Bullock
General Secretary
Division of Curriculum Resources
General Board of Education

Acknowledgments

Appreciation is expressed to the following consultants who have reviewed manuscripts and given invaluable assistance at each stage in the preparation of this manual.

DONALD B. APP
Pastor, The United Methodist Church
Torrington, Wyoming

MILO F. BENNINGFIELD
Pastor-Counselor, Family Guidance Center
Dallas, Texas

E. CRAIG BRANDENBURG
Associate Secretary, Division of Higher Education General Board of Education
The United Methodist Church
Nashville, Tennessee

DAVID BARNES CHAMBERLAIN
Psychologist
LaJolla, California

CURTIS A. CHAMBERS
Editor, *Together*
Park Ridge, Illinois

HOWARD J. CLINEBELL, JR.
Professor of Pastoral Counseling
School of Theology at Claremont
Claremont, California

HELEN F. COUCH
Editor, *The Christian Home*
Nashville, Tennessee

EUGENE M. FRANK
Bishop, Missouri Area
St. Louis, Missouri

FLORIDE MOORE GARDNER
Professor of Education
Woman's College of Georgia
Milledgeville, Georgia

WILLIAM H. GENNÉ
Coordinator, Marriage and Family Ministries
National Council of the Churches of Christ
New York, New York

C. STEDMAN GLISSON, JR.
Physician, Atlanta, Georgia

IVERSON GRAHAM, JR.
Director, Pastoral Care and Counseling
South Carolina Conference
Florence, South Carolina

BERKLEY C. HATHORNE
Coodinator, Education and Training Division of Special Mental Health Programs
National Institute of Mental Health
Chevy Chase, Maryland

GERALD K. HILL
Associate Minister, First United Methodist Church
Counselor, Mental Health and Retardation Clinic
Fargo, North Dakota

HARVEY C. HOLLAND
Chaplain, Little Rock Air Force Base
Jacksonville, Arkansas

EDWARD B. HOLLENBECK
Pastor, Asbury United Methodist Church
Little Rock, Arkansas

FRANCIS E. KEARNS
Bishop, Ohio East Area
Canton, Ohio

T. CECIL MYERS
Pastor, Grace United Methodist Church
Atlanta, Georgia

EVERETT W. PALMER
Bishop, Portland Area
Portland, Oregon

THOMAS J. PUGH
Professor of Pastoral Counseling
Gammon Theological Seminary
Atlanta, Georgia

PAUL G. SCHURMAN
Director, Program in Pastoral Care and Counseling
Ohio East Area of The United Methodist Church
Canton, Ohio

LEON SMITH
Director of Ministries in Marriage
General Board of Education
The United Methodist Church
Nashville, Tennessee

EDWARD D. STAPLES
Director of Ministries to Parents
General Board of Education
The United Methodist Church
Nashville, Tennessee

CHARLES W. STEWART
Professor of Pastoral Theology and Supervised Ministries
Wesley Theological Seminary
Washington, D.C.

TROY M. STRONG
Superintendent, Columbia River District
Pacific Northwest Conference
Wenatchee, Washington

JAMES S. THOMAS
Bishop, Iowa Area
Des Moines, Iowa

JOHN M. VAHINGER
Professor of Psychology and Pastoral Counseling
The School of Theology
Anderson College
Anderson, Indiana

W. RALPH WARD
Bishop, Syracuse Area
Syracuse, New York

DEFORREST WIKSTEN
Director, Methodist Counseling Ministry
Dallas—Fort Worth Area
Dallas, Texas

FOSTER J. WILLIAMS
Area Director, Pastoral Care and Counseling
Indiana Area of The United Methodist Church
Indianapolis, Indiana

9

BERNICE M. WRIGHT
Dean, College of Home
Economics
Syracuse University
Syracuse, New York

DONALD R. YOUNG
Director of Marriage and
Family Study and Coun-
seling Center
Institute of Religion and
Human Development
Texas Medical Center
Houston, Texas

Appreciation is also expressed to the many pastors in local
churches who have tested this manual in manuscript form.

Contents

PART I
The Context of Premarital Counseling

CHAPTER 1

Premarital Counseling Is Important

Why are you concerned about increasing your skills in premarital counseling? It is assumed that you are, or you would not be taking time to read this book. You are a busy pastor with many other urgent matters demanding your attention, and you have quite likely turned to this manual because you expect it to give you some help with your tasks.

You know that your church expects you to "hold premarital conferences, using the official manual of the Church" [1] with each couple you marry, and you want these sessions to be more than simply planning the details of the rehearsal and the wedding. You want them to be more than reading over the ritual and discussing it with the engaged couple, important as that is.

Most likely you are one of the nine-out-of-ten pastors in our church (actually, 94 percent) who insists on meeting with couples one or more times before you will marry them, for purposes other than the rehearsal. (This 94 percent is made up of 73 percent

<hr>

[1] *The Book of Discipline of The United Methodist Church,* ¶350, 5a.

who always insist on premarital sessions and 21 percent who usually do.) [2]

It may be that your are one of those who received some training in pastoral counseling in seminary, but perhaps only two or three hours of the entire course were devoted to premarital counseling. Only a little more than half of us (53 percent) have had any training in premarital counseling, either while we were in school or in workshops or seminars since leaving school. Training, for the majority of us, has been limited to only a few days at pastors' school or in a workshop. When we check on the take-home benefits of such training, less than one out of five pastors rate this training as "highly helpful," while 29 percent say it was only "moderately helpful."

Perhaps this is why more than half of us expressed a desire for more training in premarital counseling.

Some of our seminaries are now offering more training in premarital counseling, especially in short courses at summer school or as a part of a regular semester course in case studies. The Board of Education cooperates with annual conferences in providing workshops on premarital counseling and seminars in marriage counseling. For details write to the Director of Ministries in Marriage, P. O. Box 871, Nashville, Tennessee 37202.

You Want Help Now

In your case, however, you may feel that you cannot wait several months or a year for such training. You want help now. You want to do some reading and studying on your own. Of course a book cannot substitute for more adequate training through formal courses, pastoral training in an accredited setting, or clinical supervision by a well-trained counselor. But those responsible for this manual believe it can give you some guidelines in the direction of more adequate premarital counseling.

But why are you concerned about premarital counseling just now?

[2] Figures cited here and immediately following are from the study by Gerald Kingsbury Hill, "Premarital Counseling Practices and Attitudes Among Ministers of The Methodist Church" (doctoral dissertation, Teachers College, Columbia University, 1969), pp. 57-58.

Does your concern grow out of an immediate problem with a couple you are now seeing? If so, you may be tempted to turn to the section of this manual which deals with that particular subject. But remember, such an approach is likely to lead you to look for techniques or easy answers apart from basic understanding. Actually, understanding who you are, the context in which you work, and what it is you are trying to do is far more important than methods. But such understanding must grow out of your being yourself, a minister of the gospel, in relationship to people. This manual attempts to give you some help in each of these areas—a source for the methods which will best express your style of ministry.

Your motivation for improvement may also arise out of some unhappy past experience. Maybe you feel badly about the last couple you married. Maybe they had a special problem that needed attention. You knew about it, but they did not bring it up. You were not sure how to get at it. And now you are worrying about not giving them as much help as you think you should have given.

Or your feelings may go even deeper. Perhaps one of the couples you married only two or three years ago is already getting a divorce. Now you are questioning your ability as a premarital counselor. If you can keep such anxiety from driving you to despair, or causing you to grasp at straws, maybe you can direct it into constructive channels for improvement. We must not underrate the positive value of anxiety, of course, but we must remember that we are not expected to be perfect or always to get perfect results.

One of our chief weaknesses as pastors is our drive to succeed. This may cause us to try to do too much for a couple. This manual is intended to help you do your best to help a couple and to leave the rest in their hands. When you have done your best, you can commit the situation to God and trust him to continue to work in the lives of the couple.

You Care About Families

Your desire to improve your skill in premarital counseling may grow primarily out of your concern for the welfare of persons. In your various contacts with the families in your parish you may have discovered a great deal of marital unhappiness.

Some pastors estimate that from 25 to 40 percent of the persons in their congregations each Sunday are unhappy in their marriages. Although these pastoral estimates may seem high, they are not as high as those made by professional marriage counselors, who state that half the persons married today are unhappy. This is not to say that all of them are contemplating divorce. But it is to say that a large percentage of couples are struggling with difficulties severe enough to indicate that help is needed.

Even though no authentic research is yet available to support our hopes, many of us believe that premarital counseling can be an effective preventative of trouble. Not that premarital counseling is a cure-all. We know better! But we do believe that it has real value. Many couples indicate that it does and a number of authorities agree.[3]

The High Divorce Rate

The extremely high incidence of divorce may be another reason for your concern about premarital counseling. And rightly so, for the United States has the highest divorce rate of any country in the world. Of course we really do not know if premarital counseling, as presently practiced, is effective in preventing divorce. But it seems likely that it is, and therefore it is important to continue such counseling until some findings are available.

In some large cities the high divorce rate is appalling. In one metropolitan county, for example, a divorce was granted for each 1.24 marriage licenses issued in 1966.[4] Some people think these figures mean that 80 percent of the marriages in that particular county are ending in divorce. However, many young couples granted a divorce in the urban county were actually married one, two, or three years earlier in another county, perhaps in a small town or rural area.

---

[3] Aaron L. Rutledge, *Pre-marital Counseling* (Schenkman, 1966), p. xiii: "Premarital counseling is the greatest educational and clinical opportunity in the life of a person—still time to effect adult personality changes and at the same time invest in soon-to-be-born children." See also Esther O. Fisher, *Help for Today's Troubled Marriages* (Hawthorn, 1968), pp. 201-2.

[4] Bill Morgan, *Dallas Times Herald*, February 12, 1967, p. 1.

The National Center for Health Statistics estimated that in 1968 there was slightly less than one divorce to each 3.5 marriages for the nation as a whole.[5] But we must remember that this figure is for only one calendar year, and it is a partial figure. The highest divorce rate in our history is one divorce to three marriages, and this was the rate in 1946, immediately after World War II when we experienced the breakup of many war marriages. Following the 1946 peak, the divorce rate declined until 1958 when it leveled off to one divorce in four marriages. Since 1958 the divorce rate has shown a gradual increase almost every year.

More accurate, perhaps, is the ratio of divorces in any given year to the total number of marriages in our population. This ratio includes couples who married two, ten, twenty, or fifty years ago (all of whom are potential divorcing couples) and is not limited to those who marry in any one year. On this basis, in 1967 there was one divorce for each ninety marriages.[6] Such a figure compares the actual number of divorces in any one year with all the marriages that might possibly end in divorce at that time.

Children and Divorce

Many authorities used to think that children were a deterrent to divorce and cited statistics to indicate that the majority of couples getting divorces did not have children. But that was before 1957. Since then the majority of divorcing couples have had one or more children. In 1967 there were 701,000 children under eighteen years of age whose parents were divorced during that year.[7] And divorce may be much more difficult for children than for adults.

A few years ago pastors sometimes recommended that couples contemplating divorce have a baby to solve their problem. Not so any more. Now most of us realize that for a couple in conflict to have a child only adds to their problems and diminishes their resources. It also exposes a child to serious damage.

You might say "divorce runs in the family." One study found that the divorce rate was much higher among couples whose parents were divorced. If both a husband and wife came from

[5] *Monthly Vital Statistics Report*, Vol. 17, No. 12, p. 2.
[6] *Monthly Vital Statistics Report*, Vol. 18, No. 1, p. 2.
[7] *Ibid.*, p. 1.

homes where there had been *no* divorce, their divorce rate was only 14.6 percent. But if the parents of *one* of the partners had been divorced, the couple's divorce rate increased to 23.7 percent. If the parents of *both* partners had been divorced, their divorce rate climbed to 38 percent.[8]

Of course this study does not mean that children whose parents are divorced can never have a happy marriage. But it does alert us to the fact that they may need some conscientious assistance in making intelligent preparation for marriage.

While we are on the subject of divorce, perhaps we should add that teen-age marriages are especially likely to end in divorce. For example, a person who marries before seventeen is three times as likely to get a divorce as one who marries at age twenty-one. Another way to say the same thing is that approximately one-half of all teen-age marriages end in divorce. In addition, best estimates are that in one-half of all teen-age marriages the bride is pregnant before marriage.[9]

The sobering thing about teen-age marriage is that 92 percent of the weddings are performed by pastors in their home churches. This raises the question: How much premarital counseling are we doing and how helpful is it?

Most likely each time we see one of these marriages breaking up, or each time we try in vain to help a couple in conflict find their way to reconciliation and a satisfying life together, we promise ourselves that we are going to do a better job of premarital counseling with the next couple we marry.

You Care About Persons

Most of us want to do a better job of premarital counseling because we care about what happens to persons.

One of the main motivations for being in the ministry is a desire to help persons achieve a life of righteousness. We identify with Jesus' words, "I came that they may have life, and have it abun-

[8] Judson T. and Mary G. Landis, *Building a Successful Marriage* (Prentice-Hall, 1968), pp. 112-14.
[9] Robert O. Blood, *Marriage* (Free Press, 1969); *Sex Ways—In Fact and Faith*, edited by Evelyn M. and Sylvanus M. Duvall (Association Press, 1961), pp. 73-74.

dantly" (John 10:10b). We believe that the abundant life is for all persons and usually includes marriage. In fact, we see marriage as one of God's good gifts which, when accepted and used rightly, dignifies and enhances life.

We know, however, that for many, marriage is a disappointing and degrading relationship. This stimulates us to try to find better ways of enabling couples to experience a mutually satisfying life together. Premarital counseling can make an important contribution to the enrichment of marriage from the very beginning.

Marriage Is Important

Premarital counseling is important because marriage is important—both to persons and to society in general.

Persons Involved

In the first place, marriage is important because of the number of persons involved. In fact, ninety-three out of one hundred persons in this country marry at some time during their lives.[10] The National Center for Health Statistics predicted that more than four million persons would marry during 1968 alone.[11] It is estimated that nine out of ten first marriages are performed by clergymen. Obviously this presents us with a real challenge—an opportunity to minister to a large number of persons at one of the most critical periods in their lives. The question is whether ours will be a significant ministry or a superficial one.

Husbands and Wives

Secondly, marriage is important to the persons being married. Marriage is an intimate living relationship in which a man and a woman may help each other to meet their needs as persons. This includes their need for companionship and ego-support as well as their sexual needs. Marriage is an opportunity for personal fulfillment and self-realization for both partners.

Marriage does not necessarily guarantee a satisfying sexual relationship, but it does provide the socially approved framework within which couples may find their way to sexual fulfillment.

[10] Paul H. Landis, *Making the Most of Marriage* (Appleton-Century-Crofts, 1965), p. 29.

[11] *Monthly Vital Statistics Report*, Vol. 17, No. 12, p. 1.

In our society today there are so many depersonalizing influences that make us feel like numbers or cogs in machines instead of human beings. Is it any wonder then that husbands and wives are expecting more of each other than ever before, especially in the area of their personal affectional needs? Many men and women are aware of the fact that they do not really know who they are as persons until they "find themselves" in the marriage relationship. After experiencing this self-realization, these persons describe their former selfhood as incomplete, or think of themselves as having been only half-persons.

Many of us have other close interpersonal relationships to help meet our fellowship needs, as we should have, of course. But to cope with our basic sense of loneliness, most of us need the companionship in depth that a stable marriage provides. There is a real sense then in which we become whole persons as our lives are complemented by our mates, as our needs are fulfilled by our mates.

Another social factor making marriage more important to the married couple today is mobility. When young couples move away from their parents, they are more dependent on each other.

The Time Element

In addition to the quality of the relationship, marriage is also important because of the length of time a man and a woman are a married couple, as contrasted to their being children or being parents. Most people in the United States today live together as man and wife, without children in the home, longer than they were children in the parental home, or longer than they are primarily parents with their own children at home.

The average woman today is married shortly after her twentieth birthday. (Her husband is usually just about two years older.) She usually has her first child by the time she is twenty-two (from eighteen months to two years after marriage) and her last when she is twenty-six or twenty-seven. Since most children leave home at eighteen, this means that her last child is launched when she is forty-four or forty-five. With a life expectancy of sixty-eight to seventy for her husband, she has from twenty-one to twenty-four years of marriage left. Although she is a wife as well as a mother

22

during the years the children are at home, we might sum up by saying twenty years a "child," twenty-two to twenty-three years a mother (and wife), and twenty-three to twenty-six years a wife without children at home. For the family life cycle, see *Family Ministry—Through the Church* by Leon Smith and Edward D. Staples, pp. 32-33.[12]

Since our culture puts so much emphasis on parenthood and parent-child relationships, it sometimes comes as a surprise that the average couple have a longer life together without children at home than they do with children at home.

Children

Marriage is important to children, both in their development as persons and in their preparation for marriage.

Today marriage is the foundation of the family and provides the atmosphere, or climate, in which children are born and reared. For healthy development as a person, a child needs the security and warmth of a stable, loving relationship between his mother and father. Family unit therapy is revealing that children with emotional problems are often victims of troubled marriages.

For example, a person who does not find his companionship needs met by his marriage partner may turn too much attention to a child, whose life may be warped in the process. On the other hand, family unit therapy is also showing us that parent-child conflicts may contribute to marriage problems.

Positively stated, the best preparation for marriage we can give our children is a sound marriage of our own. The best preparation is not some formal instruction on how to succeed in marriage. Rather, it is the experience of living in the context of a satisfying marriage—a marriage in which partners are able both to cope with problems and tensions that seem to be inevitable in close human relationships and to enjoy the pleasures and rewards these relationships make possible. In such a climate children can learn to be themselves, free to be open and trusting. They can learn the fundamental and essential skills of communication as well as the pro-

[12] Adapted from Evelyn Millis Duvall, *Family Development* (Lippincott, 1967), p. 15. The life span continues to lengthen, especially for husbands.

cess of decision-making and problem-solving on the basis of mutually established goals and values.

At the same time, we must recognize that there are many homes today where there is only one parent in the home because of death, divorce, or separation. In such cases there must be adjustments and compensations for this situation. That is another problem, of course, and is mentioned here only to recognize that it does exist.

Society

Marriage is important to society, for marriage itself is a social institution performing certain functions for the general welfare. Since a family consists of a small group of two or more persons related by marriage, birth, or adoption, a married couple constitutes a family. Beyond this, however, marriage is the foundation of the family with children. The family is a basic unit of society. Many believe it is the primary unit.

What are some of the services of the family as a social institution? Marriage, as we have seen, is the socially approved framework in which men and women may join in meeting their needs as sexual beings.

Further, marriage is the only socially approved relationship for child-bearing. The family is responsible for bearing enough children to keep the world populated (but not overpopulated!).

The family is also an institution essential for child-rearing, meeting the child's needs for physical, emotional, social, and spiritual growth, particularly in the early years.

The family is an agency for transmitting the culture and conserving the fundamental values on which it is based. But the family not only conserves and transmits values, it also is an agent for change and improvement from one generation to another. With its provision for privacy and security for its members, the family serves as the matrix for the formation of attitudes and values, thereby shaping the very structure of our society.

Even though some social scientists believe that the family is facing a period of declining influence over members of society as compared to the influence of political and economic institutions, many others are pointing out the important values that families are contributing to society. For example, when family members are willing to sacrifice for one another and are loyal to one another because they believe loyalty is grounded in reality, to this extent society is infused with a sense of the dignity and worth of persons —a basic value. On the other hand, when family loyalty or the sacredness of the marriage is violated, family relationships are weakened, and society, in turn, loses its basic social motivation. Thus, dependable, functioning marriages contribute durability to the very fabric of society.

The Kingdom of God

Both as a structure of society and as a channel of God's love, marriage is important to the kingdom of God. In the wedding ceremony we say that marriage "is an honorable estate, instituted of God." This means that we believe marriage is a structure of human relationships given by God in creation. We believe that he ordained marriage for most persons, though there are exceptions, of course, since each person must discover God's will for himself. Therefore, marriage is one of God's good gifts to be accepted, used, and enjoyed; it is not to be misused, abandoned, or destroyed.

Marriage may also become the channel for God's love. God is the source of love, and even though he has an unlimited number of ways of coming into this world, one of the most effective is through the love of a man and a woman for each other. The marriage relationship may convey God's unconditional love—a love which sacrifices, forgives, sustains, affirms. When this love is shared not only between husband and wife, but also with their children and beyond the immediate family to others in the community and world, to this extent the kingdom of God is reality.

As stated above, premarital counseling is not a cure-all. But as one means of helping couples prepare for marriage, it is important. It has ultimate significance for the pastor who feels a keen sense of responsibility because of its opportunity for ministry to persons. This is especially true when we realize that our ministry in premarital counseling is performed in the context of the Christian faith and community.

CHAPTER 2

The Pastoral Context

The fact that we do our premarital counseling within the context of pastoral care adds some significant dimensions to our work. After all, we are pastors—ministers of the gospel—and not psychiatrists or family physicians. These unique dimensions of the pastoral context will be considered here under the topics: (1) What It Means to Be a Pastoral Counselor; (2) Expectations of the Pastor; (3) The Christian Faith and Community; and (4) The Pastor and the Couple.

What It Means to Be a Pastoral Counselor

What does it mean to you to be a pastor or minister of the gospel? How does this affect premarital counseling? This is asking the basic question: Who are you? And the equally important question: What difference does your *being* make in this aspect of your ministry?[1]

[1] Howard J. Clinebell, Jr., *Basic Types of Pastoral Counseling* (Abingdon Press, 1966), pp. 41-56.

A pastor is one who *cares* for people. This care is not only a genuine concern for all that happens to people as whole persons in all their relationships (with themselves, others, the world, history, and God), but concern which emphasizes the dimension of the spiritual and eternal in all these relationships. In fact, the overarching goal of all pastoral counseling is the spiritual growth of persons.

Shepherding Functions

This caring is expressed in action, in the shepherding functions of healing, sustaining, guiding, and reconciling.[2] In premarital counseling these functions provide different ways of bringing the whole gospel through the person and ministry of a pastor to an individual or couple contemplating marriage. The particular form of premarital counseling may involve the pastor with an individual, a couple, or group, although most often we think of the one-to-one relationship.

Healing centers around helping individuals to overcome the hurt and brokenness in their lives and become whole persons. It is obvious that very little can be done in this area in the rather limited number of interviews usually allotted to premarital counseling, but this basic concern for health and wholeness will always be present. On occasion, the pastor may be sought out several months before the wedding and given an opportunity of sharing in the growth of a person toward wholeness.

For example, a widow may be approaching a new marriage, but still have a grief problem to be worked through. Or a divorcee may have been so severely hurt in a previous marriage that healing cannot take place for months. Such persons may require depth counseling over a long period of time, which may mean the postponement of marriage.

The pastoral-care function of *sustaining* has to do mainly with supporting or strengthening a person to cope with a situation or condition that cannot be changed. This may mean helping a person to accept and adjust to a handicap or limitation, his own or the other person's. Or it may take the form of supporting one or both persons through a brief period of uncertainty—if that is all it

[2] *Ibid.*, p. 39.

27

is. Much so-called premarital panic is a form of anxiety arising from fears that have been buried. Such panic may signal the need for professional help to discover why a person is so afraid of entering marriage. In any case, we must be careful not to reassure too hastily or superficially. For if there is a real fear underlying the uncertainty, this must be dealt with directly and not be covered up.

Perhaps most of us think of premarital counseling primarily as *guiding*, that is, as being mainly instructional or educative counseling, with the pastor taking the initiative and doing most of the talking. Actually, educative counseling does include the giving of information, but it is much more than this. It is helping persons make decisions and plan for the future in the most constructive manner possible under the circumstances. In this kind of counseling the pastor does not do most of the talking; rather he assists a couple to draw on their own resources and make decisions for themselves. He tries to help them to be realistic about the many adjustments they will be making in marriage and to view these adjustments in the light of ultimate concerns of the Christian understanding of the meaning of marriage. (Chapter 9 deals with educative counseling.)

The *reconciling* function of pastoral care involves the pastor in helping a person or couple face their conflicts and reestablish their broken relationship with each other or with God. This kind of need may be the result of premarital sexual experiences or pregnancy. We do not gloss over difficulties for the couple, but face them realistically and with understanding love. Such problems usually call for forgiveness and discipline.

A Minister of the Gospel

A minister of the gospel, then, is a servant who gives his life in helping people to know the good news and to live by it. The gospel is the good news of God to man that adds the eternal dimension to all of life. Thus, as ministers, we share the redeeming love of God with those who have sinned and separated themselves from one another or from God.

As ministers of the gospel we also endeavor to uphold certain values and principles that we believe represent God's purposes expressed in marriage. This does not mean that we will be rigid and dogmatic. But it does mean we have made certain commitments and recognize certain responsibilities. We must remember always who we are and what our function is.

Specifically, when we are confronted with a decision as to whether to marry a particular couple, we must act as ministers of the gospel and not as justices of the peace. For to perform the ceremony for two persons who see marriage as no more than a temporal legal contract is a violation of our integrity as ministers. On the other hand, it would also be a violation of our integrity if we failed to make available to such a couple all the resources of the gospel and the church at this time of critical need in their lives.

Likewise, our integrity as ministers requires that we limit ourselves to our role as pastors. Thus, for instance, when the need for deep psychotherapy is indicated, we respond as pastoral counselors to the limit of our ability. But beyond that we refer the person to a psychiatrist or other competent professional. We do not attempt to go beyond our limits and act as if we are someone we are not.

Some persons would emphasize also the unique training and resources of the pastor, as contrasted with other counselors. Whereas some other counselors may be trained primarily in dealing with the inner dynamics of a person's life or in the field of interpersonal relationships, the pastor's training is usually heavily concentrated in the area of the search for meaning and value, most likely through the study of Scripture, doctrine, or church history.

The absence of training in the field of interpersonal relationships is one of the major weaknesses of ministerial education. For clergymen deal with interpersonal relationships in all aspects of their work, especially in marriage and family ministries. Even when our training includes personality development and interpersonal relationships, these are set within the larger framework of moral and spiritual values. Our training should equip us to help persons find the meaning of existence, both personal and in the whole scheme of things. This kind of training, for example, may enable us to help persons appreciate the value of the marital relationship rather than see marriage as an end in itself.

To be sure, other Christian counselors may also use the resources of the Christian faith—Scripture, prayer, sacraments, devotional literature. But, because of his office, the pastor has a special opportunity to use these resources, whenever appropriate, in his counseling—whenever appropriate, because they must never be used as a crutch or a club or as a substitute for the hard work of struggling with a problem and searching for a solution in real life.

For instance, a couple may reveal to their pastor that their reason for planning to marry is premarital pregnancy. He cannot immediately turn the couple and the problem over to God in prayer and forget about all the hard work required to find the best possible solution. Instead, supported by prayer and all the other resources of the church and the Christian faith, he guides the couple in exploring every possible alternative and in following through with one which seems best for all concerned.

Variety of Responsibilities

Undoubtedly premarital counseling is only one of many responsibilities you carry as the pastor of a congregation. This is true also if you are one of that very small but growing group of ministers today who are giving full time to counseling as a part of the staff of a large church or pastoral counseling center. At times, responsibilities may come into conflict with one another and create problems for you. How do you cope with such conflicts?

When your function as a church administrator clashes with your role as a counselor, what do you do? Take an example: As an administrator you must help make a decision regarding a young woman's continuing to serve as leader of an informal group in your youth fellowship. She is one of your most attractive and dedicated workers. You already know that she has delayed marriage until her late twenties because of the illness and financial need of her mother, now deceased. But in your premarital counseling you learn that she has been having an affair with her employer, and is wondering if she should tell her fiancé about it. She is troubled about what this might mean to him. You are concerned about her and

30

about whether she should continue to work with the young people of the church. What will you do?

Or when your preaching responsibilities threaten to undermine a counseling relationship, what do you do? It is Friday afternoon, and for once you already have your Sunday morning sermon prepared. In fact, the subject is already printed in the bulletin. You have worked hard to get it all done so you and your family can get out of town just as soon as the children are out of school, and that is only an hour from now. So as soon as you complete this counseling session, you are leaving for an overnight stay on the lake with friends. You plan to stay as long as you can and return late Saturday night.

Your counseling session is with a young man. You do not know him too well, for only the young woman he plans to marry is a member of your church. But you feel you are beginning to develop a relationship with him. This is the first session with him alone since the two of them filled out their premarital questionnaires. You have reviewed the questionnaires and discovered that a major cause of disagreement is their differing views as to whether the church should be involved in social issues. The young woman is very liberal, but the young man is conservative on this point. As the session comes to a close you suddenly realize that you have spent most of the hour (and he has spent most of his emotional energy) on this one area of conflict, and that this is exactly what you are planning to preach about on Sunday! You know the couple plans to be present. You wonder if they will think you are preaching "at them," or if you are taking sides against one of them in their conflict. It is too late to change your sermon. Or should you, even if you had time? What do you do?

Finding Time

One problem most of us face is finding time to do all that is expected of a pastor. With so many other responsibilities demanding attention, we may find it hard to schedule premarital counseling appointments. This may be especially difficult when couples work and can see us only in the evenings or on weekends.

In an interdisciplinary conference on marriage counseling, one pastor explained that he was able to solve this problem by seeing couples late in the evenings after church committee meetings. A social worker in the group criticized him severely for giving what she called the "ragged edges" of the day to premarital counseling. She said he should not be doing counseling at all if the only time he could find for it was at the end of day when he was too tired to put very much of himself into it. (Some pastors, however, feel they are able to do their best work in the evenings.)

Occasionally pastors are criticized by church officials for giving too much time to counseling. After all, it is possible to spend so much time on one part of our ministry that we do not have enough time left for other equally important tasks. Some pastors spend so much time counseling that they neglect sermon preparation or church administration responsibilities.

It may be especially difficult to find enough time for premarital counseling if several couples are to be married at about the same time. This does happen on occasion. When it does, why not take advantage of the opportunity for group premarital counseling? This approach is often more effective than seeing a couple alone—at least for some of the time.

How many weddings do you have in a year? The nationwide study already referred to found that more than a third of the ministers (35 percent) marry less than six couples a year. Almost a third (31 percent) have from six to ten weddings a year. This means that about two-thirds average less than one wedding a month. If we add to this the 17 percent who marry from eleven to fifteen couples each year, this averages about one wedding a month for 83 percent of us. Less than 13 percent of the pastors in our church have sixteen or more weddings a year.[3]

As an overall average only three-fourths of the ministers serving a church of less than nine hundred members average about one wedding a month. Usually when we have more than one wedding a month we are part of a multiple staff serving a larger congregation. If we should average four or five one-hour appointments with each couple we marry, most of us would be giving a little more than an hour a week to premarital counseling. Some couples, of course, will require more time than "the average."

[3] Hill, "Premarital Counseling Practices," p. 56.

32

Expectations of the Pastor

Because he is a pastor, couples have certain expectations with which they approach their pastor.[4] Some of these expectations are positive, others negative when related to premarital counseling. They may be based, not on personal contact or direct experience, but on a generalized conception of what couples think a pastor is supposed to be or do.

Help Is Expected

Most people expect help from their pastor. In fact, they may turn to him more often than to anyone else. Perhaps you are aware of the nationwide study a few years ago which found that one out of seven adults had sought professional help with a personal problem.[5] Forty-two percent of these went to their pastors, 29 percent to their family doctor, 18 percent to a psychiatrist or psychologist, and 10 percent to an agency such as Family Services. Of the Protestants who attend church at least weekly, the figure was even higher—54 percent went to their minister.

You may feel that it is dcfferent with premarital counseling. You may be finding it difficult to get some couples to come to you in time to schedule as many interviews as may be necessary for any depth counseling. Perhaps their expectations have something to do with their readiness to come.

An Authority Figure

Most people see their pastor as a religious authority figure. They may look up to him with a warm feeling of trust and confidence. These feelings may lead some persons to come to him with a sense of dependence, looking for "answers" or some "good advice." They may want to shift to him their responsibility for decision-making and expect him to tell them what to do. Others may react against the image of authority, strongly resisting any kind of help from him.

[4] Seward Hiltner and Lowell G. Colston, *The Context of Pastoral Counseling* (Abingdon Press, 1961).

[5] Gerald Gurin, and others, *Americans View Their Mental Health* (Basic Books, 1960), p. 307.

A Protector of Morals

Because the minister is regarded as a protector of morals of the community, he may be expected to be judgmental, condemning those who make mistakes. On the one hand, a person who feels he is "in the right" may talk very freely about a partner's wrongdoings, expecting the minister to take sides. On the other hand, a person may hesitate to "confess his sins" for fear of being condemned by the pastor. Because of this nearly universal expectation, the pastor may be the last person in the community to learn about a particular problem—such as premarital pregnancy. And many young people may be very reluctant to talk with their pastor about their sex feelings or experiences.

We need to be aware of these feelings and to discover their meaning to persons in counseling so that we can deal with them creatively, both for the growth of persons involved and for the improvement of their relationships. Otherwise we may be at sea, wondering what is going on and failing to give the constructive help that is so desperately needed.

A Married Man

As a pastor of a congregation, you are usually known to your people as a married man. Parishioners probably know your wife and have some feelings about the quality of your marriage. Young people may be encouraged to come to you for premarital counseling if they know you are happily married. Most persons, however, find it hard to accept the fact that pastors have problems, either in their personal lives or in marriage, and knowledge of such problems may deter some. The pressure to demonstrate a happy marriage may sometimes cause us to cover up problems and to refuse to seek help when we need it ourselves.

A pastor who has encountered some problem in his own marriage may be more sensitive to the needs of others, but he may be more vulnerable too. However, a pastor does not have to be perfect or free from all problems to be a good counselor. But he does have to understand himself, his needs, and his problems enough so that his problems do not control him and cause him to seek substitute satisfaction through his counseling relationships. Generally a pastor is able to be a better counselor when he is a

34

healthy, wholesome, mature person who is having his own needs met in a sound, satisfying marriage. If he is single, he finds ways of meeting his needs outside the counseling relationship.

The Place for Counseling

Closely related to their expectations of the pastor are the feelings of persons approaching counseling about the place in which counseling sessions are held. The actual physical setting has some meaning for most persons, and this meaning may facilitate or impede counseling.

Most ministers do premarital counseling in the church building, usually in the pastor's study. Some of us may be forced to use a corner of the sanctuary or a classroom. A classroom with a door that can be closed is usually better than the sanctuary. In smaller churches counseling sessions may be held in the parsonage. Any of these locations still symbolizes "the church" to most people.

What is significant here is the fact that the church building symbolizes something to each individual. For most persons the church represents God. A person who believes God is loving and forgiving is likely to respond positively to premarital counseling in the church. Another person, who conceives of God as a tyrannical judge bent on punishing offenders against his law, will react negatively—at least initially, or until firsthand experience with a pastor who is a warm, caring person changes his mind. Is it not wise, then, to be sensitive to what the church symbolizes to particular people?

The Christian Faith and Community

To do our premarital counseling in the pastoral context means that we are undergirded by the Christian faith and work as a part of the Christian community. We do not operate in a vacuum but within a definite frame of reference. We do not counsel as a lone professional but as a member of a group—the pastor of a congregation.

The Double Dimension

The Christian faith focuses on the double dimension of the divine and the human, the vertical and the horizonal relationships.

These include not only man's relationship to God as revealed in Jesus Christ, but also man's relationship to man. This double dimension provides some guides for the formulation of basic positions on faith and morality. We are concerned here especially with the implications of the Christian faith for persons in the marriage relationship. (An expanded explanation of these implications is given in Chapter 3.)

Since ours is not a creedal church demanding uniformity of belief, each pastor must think through his own position regarding such important concerns as the Christian understanding of marriage as a covenant relationship. All of us need to be aware of our basic assumptions and just how these affect our counseling. We will not want to impose our views on others, but we must be aware of our basic beliefs and why we hold them. When we are sure of our position we can permit others the freedom to find their own way. Without this kind of insight we are apt to try to influence others to believe as we do, often without realizing we are doing it.

Every counselor has some understanding of the nature of man out of which arises his style of working with people, his way of relating to others. True, he may not have thought this out very carefully. He may not be able to explain it to others with clarity. But he has some base from which he works. Awareness of this base allows him to work consistently and with some sense of direction. He is also better able to modify his basic assumptions when experience dictates that it is necessary.

In the area of morals, for example, we will operate one way if we believe that morality consists of a set of laws that have been given by God at some time in the past and are passed on to each new generation just as they are. We will operate in an entirely different way if we believe that every individual is responsible before God for his own actions and must discover God's will for him in his particular set of circumstances. What is your own position, and how do you see it influencing your counseling?

A Special Kind of Community

Closely associated with the Christian faith is the Christian community that receives, sustains, and transmits that faith. The Chris-

36

tian community is the setting for both pastor and couple. It is from this setting that the pastor works; in most instances it is also the setting in which the couple belong. In our counseling we see the man or the woman not as an isolated individual but as a member of a community—a church. Many times, of course, it may be only the woman who is actually a member of your congregation. Her fiancé may be from another community. If he is, usually he is welcomed by her friends and treated as if he actually belonged.

The church is a special kind of community, one that cares what happens to persons and to their marriages, one that shares in the significant moments in their lives, in times of crises or in high moments of celebration and rejoicing. It is a community that shares, to some extent at least, a common set of values and experiences a sense of fellowship and common purpose.

The church may show its concern for a couple by providing opportunities that will help them in preparing for marriage, in celebrating the event, and in continuing to enrich the marriage.

The church may help persons prepare for marriage through the ongoing program-curriculum either in week-by week teaching/learning experiences, or through certain events planned especially for those anticipating marriage. These may include discussion groups in the youth fellowship or in church school classes, and leaders may make use of a variety of resources, such as books and films. Groups may consider such subjects as understanding oneself, the meaning of sexuality, ethics of sex, dating and courtship, and the meaning of marriage. Such an informal group or "personal growth group" for young people is an important aid to personal maturation which will be helpful in all relationships, including marriage. In addition, the church may provide more formal courses or weekend retreats on preparation for marriage, or group counseling sessions for engaged couples. And, of course, there is premarital counseling!

The church also makes a great deal over the wedding ceremony as a high moment of celebrating a marriage. The church sees the wedding as a service of worship in which two persons take their vows before God in the presence of the congregation. This emphasizes the religious significance of the event as the formal initiation of the couple into a new state of life—"holy matrimony."

The wedding also focuses attention on the sacredness of marriage as a covenant relationship.

The Christian community helps to sustain a couple in their life together by providing continuing enrichment of their marriage across the years. The church recognizes the two persons as a married couple in a variety of ways. For example, a special group may be provided for them, such as a church school class or couples' club for married young adults. These groups afford couples the opportunity to work together to resolve some of the issues and problems with which they are struggling. The church may also provide special study in the form of fellowship events that center specifically on enriching and strengthening marriage, such as a weekend retreat in the form of a marriage communication laboratory.

Although very little is said about it today, the Christian community still has a disciplinary function. This is manifested in the expectation that a couple will honor their vows and uphold each other in love. To be sure, this is not discipline in the punitive sense; instead, it is discipline through nurture and instruction, as the couple find their life together in the congregation, or as they take advantage of helpful resources.[6] And, if trouble should come, the services of the pastor are available for marriage counseling. In fact, more than half the counseling the average pastor does involves marriage problems.

The Christian community also helps a couple to keep from making an idol of their marriage. The church challenges a couple to look beyond their own immediate needs and satisfactions, to see themselves as the church in the community where they live, and to live in the world with a sense of mission in fulfilling God's purposes for them as a married couple.

The Pastor and the Couple

One of the distinguishing qualities of premarital counseling is the relationship of the pastor and the couple. For other pro-

[6] One such resource is the monthly magazine *The Christian Home*, designed primarily for parents; it is a publication of Board of Education of The United Methodist Church. The church also provides special units of study on the meaning of marriage.

fessionals the counseling relationship is the sole relationship between the counselor and the couple. For pastors, however, there are actually three stages of relationship—before, during, and after counseling—each of which is a phase of the continuing pastoral care relationship.

An Existing Relationship

When a woman calls her pastor "to set the date for the wedding," the contact may open the way for premarital counseling. Sometimes this is their first contact, but the caller probably has known her pastor through the worship services of the church. From his sermons she already has formed some opinion as to the kind of person he is. This may be true of the man as well. Very often, however, because of the custom of having the wedding in the bride's church, the groom may be from another community.

In some cases both the man and the woman may be unknown to the pastor. But this is usually the exception rather than the rule. It is more likely to happen in downtown city churches or in churches in county-seat towns where marriage licenses are issued. Nevertheless, there is a kind of relationship, generalized perhaps from previous contacts with other pastors in years past. Most persons have some kind of notion as to what pastors are like and from this they draw their own conclusions about what premarital counseling with a pastor will be like, whether such conclusions are accurate or not.

On the other hand, the contacts between the pastor and the couple may have been rather extensive and in a variety of settings. He may have visited in the home, perhaps on a get-acquainted basis or, more likely, at a time of crisis in the family. The couple may have known him in a number of groups in the church. Some of these contacts may have been formal, others very informal. In some instances the pastor may have shared in the leadership of a preparation-for-marriage group to which the couple has belonged. These earlier contacts, whatever they were, have established some kind of relationship between the pastor and the couple. And these can influence the counseling relationship, either positively or negatively.

39

The Counseling Relationship

When the pastor has had a prior relationship with a couple, he must remember that the nature of the relationship changes when they move into counseling. He must now shift from one level of relationship to another, or add a new dimension to the former relationship, and must help the individual or couple to do the same. This may be difficult for some couples, but it is the pastor's responsibility to differentiate and clarify the nature of the new relationship.

In premarital counseling the nature of the relationship changes because of its purpose, content, process, and structure. *The purpose of the new relationship is to help a couple prepare for marriage.* This is much more direct and specific than most relationships. The goal is to help this particular couple prepare for marriage. This is not preparation for marriage generally, but for *their marriage.* Usually this is their marriage, not sometime in the distant future, but soon, which may add a sense of immediacy or urgency to the relationship.

The content of the premarital counseling session is *their lives and relationship, their problems and plans*—not research findings from the experiences of others. The focus is on their feelings and attitudes, their values and dreams. What is of crucial importance are their strengths and weaknesses, their capacities or handicaps. This means that the pastor-couple relationship is more intimate and personal than most others, for it deals with private and confidential matters not usually shared. At best, there is an openness and honesty about the relationship, a free sharing of problems and concerns. Of course there will be times when individuals or couples are not ready to talk about certain things. Some may be embarrassed or afraid. But in the counseling relationship it is the pastor's responsibility to do all he can to provide a climate of trust that will encourage those he is counseling to feel free to express their deep feelings, whether positive or negative.

On the surface the counseling may appear to be only conversation, much of which is initiated by the pastor. To be sure, there may be some instruction by the pastor, but most of the time he will be trying to ask the right questions and listen to the feelings and the meanings behind the words. He will be trying to help the individuals understand themselves and their needs, their relationships and circumstances. He does this to assist them in making their own plans or in solving their problems themselves.

The relationship between the pastor and the couple in premarital counseling then is a relationship which is distinctly different from other relationships. For one thing, it is strictly confidential. The couple needs to know that premarital counseling is limited in time and place to the set interviews in the pastor's study or other designated place. They need to be assured that every time he sees them—whether in the congregation, in a committee meeting, or on the street—he is not reviewing the details of their last counseling session. This is especially true when premarital counseling involves problems.

Although the pastor disciplines himself not to take the counseling experience out of the office with him, it is very difficult for the couple to do the same. They are likely to be self-conscious and sensitive about even unintentional references or situational elements. Thus it may be best to avoid extended social contacts with some couples during counseling. But it is foolish to talk about a pastor trying to cut off all other relationships with a couple. As a pastor you would not ask a couple to drop out of all church activities where you might be present, would you? A pastor simply cannot isolate his counseling from all other relationships, nor should he. He will continue to see his couples on various occasions.

The important thing, of course, is for the pastor not to worry about any contact outside the counseling appointments, but to make clear to the couple that counseling is a different kind of relationship.

A Continuing Relationship

After the counseling is concluded, the couple is not left entirely alone. They may be supported by the Christian community, as already indicated. In addition, they may have a continuing relationship with the pastor as members of the congregation. But if the counseling is at all helpful, that pastoral care relationship will most likely be on a much deeper level afterward. In any case, it is important for the pastor to help the couple shift gears from the counseling relationship into whatever other relationships are continuing. They need to know that the counseling is concluded, even though the possibility of reopening it is always there should the need arise.

At the conclusion of counseling, most couples will know that they have a pastor who really cares about them and is able to give them help if they should ever need it. It is very reassuring to them to know that the counseling relationship may be renewed at any time when help is needed.

Some couples, however, may need guidance in how to renew the counseling relationship. They may expect to receive tidbits of help whenever they see the pastor. It might be more accurate to say that as pastors we need to be sensitive to signals for help and guide the person or couple into counseling. Of course we must avoid making a major case out of every comment, or being too eager to get a couple to come in for counseling. But we do need to learn how to gauge the seriousness of need and to know when to suggest an appointment, or when to leave a situation alone.

If a serious moral problem should be revealed in counseling, a pastor may be concerned about his relationship with the person after the counseling is concluded. Experience seems to indicate that the continuing pastoral care relationship is weakened or endangered only when the counseling was not helpful, the problem was not resolved, or the guilt was not relieved. On the other hand, even when counseling is not effective in resolving problems, the relationship may not be affected adversely *if* the pastor was seen as understanding and helpful.

There have been instances when the situation was so very unpleasant or the necessary revelation of details so painful that persons did not want to be reminded of it even by seeing the pastor at church each week. Some such sensitive persons may not attend church for awhile until the wound heals. Or they may go to another church or actually move their membership. In some cases this last may be the best solution.

Our responsibility is to do the very best we can in counseling and not worry about the consequences in terms of attendance or church membership. If we are so afraid of losing members that we limit the depth of our counseling, then it is probably best for the couple that we do not get very deep anyway.

It is well to remember, however, that a sudden change in a person's church attendance habits, either by absence or presence, can be a clue to some personal or family need that may call for some form of pastoral care. Although there is no clear research on the subject, the best clinical judgment is that we do not have to worry about our continuing relationship with those persons who are truly helped to work through their problems, regardless of depth. Genuine expressions of concern strengthen the continuing pastoral care relationship and keep the couple aware of the availability of this concern for their well-being.

CHAPTER 3
Toward a Theology of Marriage

Since our premarital counseling is done in the   context of the Christian faith, it is well for us to explore some of our basic theological assumptions regarding marriage. Of course each pastor must work out his own theological position as a base for his ministry through premarital counseling.

The purpose of this chapter is to help you think through your own position. For premarital counseling is not a set of techniques to be used in isolation from our basic beliefs or from our vocation as Christian pastors. Premarital counseling is a form of Christian ministry, set within a framework of the Christian understanding of the nature of God, of man and, specifically, of marriage. What follows here is an attempt to describe as briefly as possible some of the basic theological assumptions on which this manual is written.

The Christian Faith

Essentially the Christian faith is not simply a statement of beliefs nor an intellectual assent to a body of doctrine. Rather, it is

44

living in the faith relationship with God within the context of the Christian community. It is trusting God as an act of one's entire being. It is responding in faith and love to God as revealed in Jesus Christ, thus permitting God's love to find expression in all the relationships of life, including those between husband and wife and their relationships with others.

Christian Morality

Since marriage requires many decisions regarding right and wrong, we need to give consideration to the nature of Christian morality. The theme of morality is human conduct, but it does not begin with man; it begins with God. Righteousness has its origin in God and comes to man as God's command. This means that Christian morality is an expression of faith growing out of one's relationship with God. It is not a separate study of conduct on the human level, but an integral part of the meaning of the Christian faith and life.

Christian morality, therefore, does not consist of a set of rules for living, nor of certain standards of conduct issued once and for all at some time in the past. God's command is always specific and concrete. Thus it cannot be stated as a rigid principle, for this would result in a legalistic ethic. However, we readily admit that man as a sinful human creature needs some kind of formulation of rules or laws not only to guide him in conduct, but to lead him to Christ, so that in Christ he may come to "righteousness through faith" (Galatians 3:24; Romans 10:4).

Further, if God's command is always specific and concrete, then true Christian morality is the will of God for a particular person living within his unique complex of relationships, in his peculiar set of circumstances, and at his particular time in history. This dynamic relational concept of morality leaves the way open for change.

Personal Responsibility

Such an understanding of morality means that each person is responsible for discovering God's will for him in his time and place—in each event—using the best insights available from all sources.

On the other hand, we recognize that we must be protected from a fanatic individualism which mistakes our own desires for God's will or which equates the two. We are afforded this protection by a careful weighing of the command of God as it comes to us in the Scriptures and in the continuing revelation of the Holy Spirit. This is a careful weighing of the Word and the Spirit as the past is applied in the present.

A further protection is afforded by the Christian community as the context in which this understanding of the will of God is worked out, for the Christian community can serve to correct and can help to guide the individual in his search. (The small sharing group is one way of doing this.) But an imperfect Christian community—made up of sinners as it always is in this world—must not become a coercive structure controlling the individual. For each person must always be left free to respond to the will of God for himself. On the other hand, the individual cannot be left "completely free" to disregard Scripture, experience, and tradition, nor the insights and welfare of others. He must weigh all of these carefully whenever he considers making a decision. As Christians we believe that the one God is at work both within the individual and within the Christian community to bring a coherence and wholeness to our understanding of the Christian way of life for all. This calls for a continuing close relationship with God for each person, whether he is a pastor or one of the marriage partners.

Faith in God

Fundamental to the Christian faith is our understanding of God, which may be stated briefly under the three persons of the Trinity—God as Father, God as Son, and God as Holy Spirit.

In the first we see God as the creator of all that is. Nothing exists apart from him. He is the "ruler and maker of all things," including man and marriage. All of life is dependent on him. Creation is not a closed event but continues in the present and into the future.

When we say we believe in "God the Son," we mean that God was in Christ, revealing himself, his love, his will. The self-giving, victorious love of God is seen especially in the life, death, and resurrection of Jesus. God reveals himself in many ways, but su-

46

premely in Jesus Christ. This is why we call ourselves Christian and seek to realize the Christian quality of life in marriage.

Through the Holy Spirit, God continues to work in the life of the individual and in marriage as well as within the church. It is through the Spirit that God continues to give us the direction and power we need to live in his love and to do his will in all things. We are not alone. God continues with us in the midst of all the perplexities and problems of life.

Two other observations are in order at this point. One is that God is the God of all life. Hence there is no distinction between sacred and secular, for God is concerned about every aspect of life, including what we call the most mundane. Nothing is outside his love and care. The other observation is that God is the God of all truth, including the insights from sociology, psychology, education, and other disciplines, as well as theology. Christians are under obligation to try to understand and use all such knowledge which is compatible with their understanding of the Christian faith.

Man and His Life in This World

At the risk of oversimplifying, some fundamental Christian beliefs about man and his life in this world that have special significance for marriage are listed here.

1. Man is a creature of God, created for the kingdom of God, and every person is of such worth that he must be treated with dignity and respected as a child of God.

2. Although man is limited and controlled by certain "givens" in his background and circumstances, essentially he is a free and responsible creature, who may be obedient to God's will for him, or may turn away from God in sin, which he often does.

3. Man is a whole person who must be understood in all dimensions of his being—body, mind, and spirit, all interrelated. He cannot be understood adequately in any one dimension alone.

4. In spite of his rebellion against God, man can become aware of his condition, turn, respond to God, and receive the redemption offered in Jesus Christ. By the gift of God's grace he can become "in Christ . . . a new creation" (2 Corinthians 5:17; Ephesians 2:8-10).

5. Man has certain physical, emotional, and social needs which

47

must be met, but essentially man is a creature in search of meaning. He wants to know what is good, true, beautiful; he has an insistent urge to know the significance of his life in terms of ultimate values. To become a fully authentic or adequate person he must find a true sense of personal meaning for himself and the whole scheme of things.

6. Life is not fixed. Change is possible even though it is often difficult and sometimes seemingly impossible. In spite of past history and present conditions God works in the lives of individuals and families to restore broken relationships and bring them to wholeness of life.

7. Man is a dependent creature who cannot exist apart from God. His very existence depends on God's providential care. He can know himself truly only in relationship to God. He can overcome the profound evils of life and realize the abundant life only through the grace of God.

8. Man is a social being who cannot live in isolation from other people. His life depends on intimate relationships with a few persons. His full development as a person will be arrested without wholesome relationships with other people.

9. Although the total demands of the kingdom cannot be fulfilled on earth, the kingdom of God may be realized in this world, at least to an extent far beyond what we now know. Christians are under obligation to acknowledge and demonstrate the reign of God in all areas of life in society.

10. Man's life is not limited to this present world. Because we believe in the triumph of life over death, we live for ultimate values and abide in the Christian hope.

Marriage Understood Theologically

Against the above background, then, marriage can be understood theologically—in relation to God and his purposes for his people; in terms of the creative, redemptive, and sanctifying work of God.

In terms of the *creative work of God*, marriage is one of those structures of society given as a part of creation. This means that marriage is viewed by Christians as a form of human relationship which God ordained for mankind generally and not alone for Christians. Hence God's intention in the very structure of society applies to all men whether they acknowledge God or not. Marriage, then, is not a convenient pairing of men and women contrived by society, but the basic social structure given by God in creation.

God's redemptive activity, however, applies to Christians, to those who are redeemed in Christ. In redemption God forgives sin and restores man to right relationship with himself and others; he becomes "in Christ . . . a new creation." Thus, when Christians come to marriage, they come as new creatures in Christ seeking to be obedient to God's will for them as persons and as a couple.

In the *sanctifying work of God,* man has the possibility of being purified and made holy, with his life centered in God. This is an opportunity for husbands and wives to respond to the work of the Holy Spirit as they "grow in grace" and "go on to perfection" by "being made perfect in love." Although problems will still plague them, in the process they will find their marriage infinitely blessed.

A Structure of Creation

As a structure of creation, marriage is understood as having an essential nature and certain purposes which apply to all marriages and not alone to marriages of two Christians.

The four purposes, or functions, of marriage are union, fellowship, procreation, and the nurture of children. They are listed chronologically—in the order in which they normally arise—for it would be a mistake to try to assign a value order to these functions. Each one is of unique importance.

One purpose of marriage is seen in its *unitive,* or *creative,* function. When two people marry they create a new unity without, of course, losing their own individuality in the process. Marriage is, in fact, an intimate relationship in which two individuals give up their independence to find their individuality strengthened and developed by their union. Male and female become "one" in marriage.

Jesus referred to the creation (Genesis 2:24) when he said "The two shall become one" (Matthew 19:5). This does not mean one

49

physical body, but a new dynamic unit—a new functioning, living, growing unity. The mystery is deep and difficult to understand; nevertheless, it is a fact. This new union may begin tentatively during courtship but is initiated radically in sexual intercourse. Of course it involves much more than sexual union, for it is a union of two whole persons, including the physical, mental, and spiritual aspects of their whole being.

Another purpose of marriage is *fellowship*, sometimes called the re-creative function. God created man, male and female—persons who are incomplete in themselves alone. In the Genesis account of the creation, "The Lord God said, 'It is not good that man should be alone'" (Genesis 2:18). God instituted marriage as a means of overcoming this aloneness, this incompleteness of individuality, and for meeting the need of man and woman to complement and fulfill each other. Marriage emphasizes man's need for intimacy and community, and it helps to meet the continuing need for recreating and nourishing the fellowship between husband and wife.

This relationship encompasses the total companionship needs of men and women, including the sexual union. Sex is one of God's good gifts to man to be used within marriage to fulfill his several purposes, including mutual satisfaction of the needs of both husband and wife. Sex is not sin, as some people believe, but it may be used for sinful, exploitative purposes either in marriage or outside. Sex is good when it meets the needs of persons and nourishes companionship, when it helps to strengthen and deepen the sense of fellowship between husband and wife as whole persons.

A third purpose of marriage is *procreation*. It is within marriage, we feel, that God intends for life to be conceived and children to be brought into the world. This is the way God plans for continuing the population. With all our concern about population expansion today, however, perhaps we need to emphasize that the admonition to "be fruitful and multiply" does not mean to overpopulate.

Since marriage is a structure of creation, we believe that all people are under obligation to use the best available knowledge and materials for family planning in keeping with God's will for them.

Specifically, The United Methodist Church holds that "responsible family planning, practiced in Christian conscience, fulfills the will of God." [1] This means that each couple must discover the will of God for them at a particular time and place, taking into account all pertinent considerations such as the physical, emotional, economic, and social factors and not simply their own personal wishes.

A fourth purpose of marriage is sometimes referred to as the *educative* function. It is our view that parents are not only to bring children into the world but also to be responsible for their protection and nurture. This is the primary, but not exclusive, obligation of parents, since they need to be assisted by other persons and agencies.

Indeed it is the responsibility of parents to make the fullest possible use of all appropriate agencies, and it is society's responsibility to see that parents neither neglect their children nor deny them the benefits of society. Christians emphasize the fact that the educative function of marriage includes the spiritual nurture of children as well as the supplying of their physical, psychological, social, educational, and other needs for full growth.

The Nature of Marriage

As to the nature of marriage, we believe that marriage should be a monogamous, lifelong union based on love and fidelity. Support for this view is found in our Christian understanding of God's purposes in creation.

Even though there may be societies in which other forms of marriage are practiced, such as in early Hebrew history when the Old Testament patriarchs were polygamists, we believe that God intends marriage to be *monogamous*. This idea is expressed in our marriage ritual in the words, "forsaking all other keep thee only unto her (or him) . . . ."

In the unitive function, for example, one man and one woman come together to establish a new union, revealed in part through

[1] *The Book of Resolutions of The United Methodist Church*, 1968, p. 91.

union in sexual intercourse. This sex act involves the person of husband and wife in a relationship of "oneness."

Likewise, the fellowship function of marriage requires one man and one woman to overcome the incompleteness of their maleness and femaleness and to meet the continuing needs of husband and wife for their mutual support and individual fulfillment. Together they nourish an intimate relationship in which they "belong" to each other exclusively—so exclusively that the entry of a third party is regarded as an intrusion and a threat to the union itself.

The necessity of monogamy is also seen in the procreative function of marriage. Each person is the child of one father and one mother, so that not only a person's physical organism, but also his very existence as a person is bound up irrevocably with two other existences, and two others only. All three are bound together indissolubly in the divine structure of creation, not as objects, but as subjects, in a unique relationship as no other three persons ever have been or ever will be bound together.

Similarly, the educative function of marriage also requires the cooperative efforts of a mother and a father. To give a child the care and protection he needs throughout childhood, his mother and father need to be united in a mature and responsible relationship.

We also believe that marriage is a *lifelong union* to be ended only by death of one of the partners. We understand that, in principle, permanence is God's will for all marriages, even though some may fall short of it in practice. The concept of the permanence of marriage is inherent in the very idea of marriage itself, since it is based on the irrevocable nature of the structure of existence given in creation. In reality, a marriage entered into on a temporary basis is no marriage at all. Further, fidelity is a necessary basis for marriage, and must be a permanent quality and not a conditional element in true marriage.

Our United Methodist wedding ritual expresses this principle of permanence both positively and negatively: "so long as you both shall live," and "till death us do part." This does not mean that marriage is to be maintained only as long as it is convenient or pleasing to do so, but for life. In fact, the couple is reminded that difficulties may be expected: "for better, for worse, for richer, for poorer, in sickness and in health."

True marriage involves a depth of companionship that cannot grow in an unstable, temporary atmosphere. It can be developed only within a permanent relationship. Further, since marriage is the foundation of the family it must furnish a durable and stable basis for bearing and rearing children. The fact that some marriages must be terminated for grave and sufficient reasons does not change the fact that the intention with which two people enter marriage must be "till death us do part."

Divorce and Remarriage

When Jesus was asked about divorce he definitely expressed the intention of permanence, even from creation: "He who made them from the beginning made them male and female . . . and the two shall become one . . . . So they are no longer two but one. What therefore God has joined together, let no man put asunder" (Matthew 19:4-6). See also Mark 10:6-9.

This statement of Jesus we recognize as the ideal but not necessarily as a binding decree on every person, for we do not believe that he was laying down a legalistic requirement to be applied rigidly in every case. Such a position would be contrary to the general character of his teachings. To say that man's choices may contribute to marriage breakdown does not mean that divorce is God's intention; this may be only recognition of a fact in the human situation. Furthermore, insistence on the absolute indissolubility of marriage in every case may be legalistic misuse of a well-intentioned principle. Such legalism fails to recognize the moral right of the exceptional case.

Several other reasons for this view can be cited. One is that we believe God is superior to his creation, that his will is supreme; therefore he is not bound by a structure of society given in creation. We believe further that God wills what is best for the welfare of persons, and what is best for one may not always be best for another.

Another reason for this view is that marriage, like any other social relationship, must be evaluated in terms of what it does to the persons involved—all persons, including children. Thus in par-

53

ticular instances separation or divorce may be the best possible solution to a marriage that is destroying the persons involved.

More important, however, God's forgiving love as we know it in Jesus Christ leads us to believe that a person need not be forever doomed by a mistake, even one involving marriage, but that he may experience God's forgiveness and become a new creature, capable of entering into a new marriage as a new person.

Remarriage after divorce (or after death, for that matter) should come only after sufficient time has passed for a person to overcome the hurt of the past and prepare for the new marriage. *The Book of Discipline of The United Methodist Church* (Paragraph 350. 5b) states: "In view of the seriousness with which the Scriptures and the Church regard divorce, he [the pastor] may solemnize the marriage of a divorced person only when he has satisfied himself by careful counseling that (1) the divorced person is sufficiently aware of the factors leading to the failure of the previous marriage, (2) the divorced person is sincerely preparing to make the proposed marriage truly Christian, and (3) sufficient time has elapsed between the divorce and the contemplated marriage for adequate preparation and counseling."

Love and Fidelity

In our marriage ceremony both the man and the woman promise "to love and to cherish" the partner. This means that love is recognized as an essential element in each function of marriage: husband and wife are united in love; their fellowship is deepened in love; they enter into procreation in love; they fulfill their educative function in love. Historically, we may have been late in recognizing love as a basis for marriage; and even today love may be lacking in many relationships. Yet in the New Testament the love of Christ for the church is compared to love in the marriage relationship. (Ephesians 5:21-33.) We see it, then, as an essential element in Christian marriage.

But love alone is not enough. Love must be combined with loyalty or fidelity to give a firm foundation for marriage. In fact, fidelity is a necessary element in genuine love; without fidelity there can be no genuine love and no true marriage. Both love and fidelity are essential to the performance of each of the functions of

54

marriage—union, fellowship, procreation, and education. Loyalty is seen in the partners' faithfulness to the marriage covenant before God as well as to each other. This involves sexual fidelity, as well as a common loyalty that protects the two from all possible interference from others who might damage any aspect of their total marriage relationship.

Christian Vocation

For the Christian, marriage and family life are understood not only as beginning in the natural creation, but also as coming within the scope of redemption, as continuing and finding fulfillment in the Christian way of life. When one becomes a Christian he is not freed from these structures of creation but is empowered to live within them, as "in Christ, a new creation." Entering marriage, for a Christian, is entering a Christian vocation and a covenant relationship.

The concept of Christian vocation has two essential elements: It begins with God's call and results in man's response. Man's response, of course, may be either acceptance or rejection. The Christian responds in love as a faithful and obedient son.

When vocation is understood broadly, it may be said that there is only one vocation or calling for the Christian, and that is discipleship. A Christian is one who has committed his entire life, his whole person, and all his relationships to God in Christ. In discipleship he tries to follow Jesus' teaching and example in all the relationships of his life.

Since God's will is always for a particular person in a particular situation, God calls each person to a specific vocational role in relation to sexuality. There are four recognized forms this vocation may take for the Christian. (1) For most persons, that vocation is marriage and parenthood. (2) For some, it may be marriage without parenthood. (3) For a few, the sexual vocation may be celibacy—the lifelong abstinence from marriage and sexual relations. Protestants insist that celibacy is not a higher calling than marriage or parenthood but may be chosen when the circumstances of a person's whole life are exceptional. (4) Continent witness may be the sexual stance of other single pesons (in addition to those who choose celibacy). This may be for a period of time prior to marriage or after a person is widowed, or it may be necessitated by the fact that he remains unmarried for a long lifetime through no choice of his own.

For those who are single, we believe it is God's will that they remain continent. There are also occasional situations where one partner or the other leads a continent role within marriage because of the extended illness of the other partner. When a person chooses continent witness as a vocation he is not doomed to an empty, fruitless life, but he finds a way to positive fulfillment as a whole person in community. Likewise, when seen in terms of God's will for the totality of one's life, no one of these four sexual roles is a denial of life, but is the fulfillment of God's purposes for that person at that particular time.

Although marriage is ordained for people generally, it is not a command from God applying to all individuals alike. Rather it is a state of life which one may choose. When a Christian chooses marriage he does so responsibly, seeking to be faithful to God's will for him in this relationship as in every other area of life.

This means that a mature, sensitive Christian does not drift into marriage; rather he chooses it as a deliberate decision of his whole being in response to God's call to marriage as a new state in life. Furthermore, he does not enter marriage with just any person to whom he may be attracted, but with that particular person with whom he sincerely believes he can fulfill God's will. This does not imply that there is only one person in the whole world whom he should marry; rather, that God's will is always expressed in a particular situation, for a particular person in his peculiar set of circumstances at a certain time; and that it is the responsibility of the Christian to discover God's will and respond to it.

Love may draw two persons toward each other, but they will not permit themselves to be overwhelmed by it. Their love for each other will lead a Christian couple to consider carefully every aspect of their relationship—physical, emotional, social, economic, as well as religious. In preparing for marriage they will use every appropriate resource, such as medical or financial advice, as well as premarital counseling by their minister. See *To Love and to Cherish* (For Engaged Couples).

A Covenant Relationship

Christian marriage is not simply a personal choice between two individuals; it is not merely a legal contract or a social institution; nor is it just a Christian ceremony prescribed by the church. Rather, Christian marriage is a covenant relationship which combines the three essential elements of the personal, social, and sacred.

The first element of the covenant relationship is *personal*. For the Christian, marriage originates in the call of God to particular individuals. Thus responding to God, two persons enter the marriage relationship on the basis of free consent. There can be no coercion of any kind. The covenant relationship is based on the personal choice of two people freely responding to God's will for them.

Another essential element of the covenant relationship is *social*. Although personal and private in origin, marriage can never be a private association regulated only by the personal desires of two individuals. Social responsibility is intrinsic to every marriage; for good or ill, society's welfare is involved in every marriage. In our culture we recognize that marriage is a social institution having such profound effect on the total social structure that society has a right to regulate it for the common good.

The public character of Christian marriage is attested to by the fact that a couple enters into the covenant relationship in the presence of the congregation. Moreover, the Christian community is concerned enough to provide the kind of preparation for marriage that will assist couples in discovering and living by the will of God for them, not only within their marriage, but also in the world, as they endeavor to fulfill their common discipleship.

The third element of the covenant relationship is its *sacred* nature. The sacredness of marriage does not lie in the fact that it is instituted in a religious ceremony before the Christian community, as important as this is, but in the fact that in Christian marriage two persons make a lifelong commitment to each other in the presence of God. God is not some external attachment added to the wedding ceremony against the will of the participants; he enters into the marriage in and through the lives of the partners.

Before God they make an unconditional covenant with each other to live in his steadfast love and to be faithful to each other and to their vows.

A Mutual Ministry

In Christian marriage there is both the covenant and the relationship. The couple enters into the covenant in the marriage ceremony, but they fulfill it in relationship. The relationship is a quality of living which may be achieved only after years of life together.

In this covenant relationship husbands and wives perform a mutual ministry of self-giving; they accept each other for better or for worse and enter into a new kind of belonging to each other. Although marriage is not considered a sacrament in The United Methodist Church, it does have a sacramental character, for God not only is in the origin and institution of the marriage, but also is a constant source of strength and guidance throughout the covenant relationship.

A Christian couple will continue in marriage not simply because of the external pressures of society or the internal personal satisfactions, but essentially because they affirm marriage as a sacred covenant relationship based on Christian love and fidelity.

This does not mean that a man and woman are bound to maintain an empty form of marriage after all life and spirit have gone out of it. Instead it means that to the best of their ability they will contribute to the growth and enrichment of their relationship so that it continues to bless their lives.

It should be noted here that the spirit does not go out of a marriage all at once. Rather this is a process of slow death, and there are many danger signals along the way. The counseling minister must help couples see that they have an obligation to be alert to these danger signals and react to them constructively. He will urge them to do their best to work out difficulties in understanding and love, allowing the redemptive grace of God to work in their lives and relationship.

A Channel for God's Love

As husbands and wives respond to the grace and love of God, their marriage is opened to infinite possibilities. Nevertheless, they are still human, still sinful, and they will continue to have problems. But now they can face their difficulties with a new spirit and a new power. Under the ministry of the Holy Spirit, couples can experience their marriage relationship as a channel for God's love.

The fact that man has been redeemed does not mean that he is thereby made perfect. He is still a sinful human creature who needs to grow in grace and love. Unless he permits God to continue to work in his life and relationships, he will regress. Man's life is potential; he ever remains open to both the demonic and the divine. Progress toward perfection, for the individual or for the couple, never comes automatically, but it does come to those who open their lives to God and respond to his guidance.

As pastors we must be realistic, however, and recognize that even the redeemed will probably have many problems that must be faced and overcome. A Christian marriage, for example, is not one in which there are no problems, but one in which the partners are trying to find Christian solutions. This means that husbands and wives must be open continually to the inspiration of the Holy Spirit. They must cooperate fully with God in removing from their lives all that causes difficulties and hinders the full expression of his love through them.

The very fact that married couples still know themselves to be sinful human creatures who have experienced God's redeeming love before, encourages them to confess their sins and to accept again God's forgiving love and to follow his guidance for the future. When they do, God enables them to express forgiving love to those who have wronged them. Further, because they have experienced God's grace before, and trust God to be at work for wholeness, they find strength to face their problems and to do their best to solve them.

Under the guidance of God's spirit a man or a woman is enabled to take a patient and generous attitude toward the marriage partner. Without being unrealistic each can see his partner in terms of his highest possibilities and be optimistic about their future. We know that God works toward overcoming conflict and achieving reconciliation, that God guides and empowers persons to seek solutions to their problems. But if they are unable to handle their problems on their own, they should be encouraged to seek competent help from an appropriate qualified source. Above all, married couples should be guided to allow God's spirit to work in their lives and relationships to restore and make whole again.

When couples respond positively to the stimulation of God's spirit, marriage becomes a channel for the expression of God's love—unconditional, sacrificing, forgiving, sustaining, affirming love. Under the influence of God's love the events of everyday life of families, in prosperity or adversity, become a "means of grace" to help persons to "go on to perfection." Not that persons become perfect in the sense of being free from sin or the problems of everyday life; but that they "grow in grace" so that they seek to become "perfect in love," always seeking to let God's steadfast love find full expression in all their relationships—within their marriage and beyond to the whole family of God. This is not so much a matter of always striving to do one's best. This persons will do, of course. But in it all they are aware of the fact that God is the source of their love, that he is at work in and through them.

Marriage Not the Ultimate Good

The more we become aware of God's love at work within us and our marriage, the more we realize that marriage is not the ultimate good. It is important, to be sure, but its importance is in the fact that it is a structure of life which God has instituted for the benefit of persons. The ultimate value in this life is always God's will and never a human relationship. The claims of the kingdom transcend those of marriage. The Christian faith affirms marriage but limits its significance.

Such an understanding of the significance of marriage keeps us from making an idol of our relationship, from believing that marriage is the most valuable thing in the world or that one's highest purpose in this life is to live for a husband or wife. It reminds us to keep marriage within the context of the reign of God in the world, so that God's will is always supreme both in the life of the individual and the couple as well.

PART II
Purpose and Content

CHAPTER 4

Marriage and Self-Understanding

Under the overall purpose of helping a couple prepare for marriage, what specific goals do you try to achieve in premarital counseling?

If you are sure about your purposes, and have them fairly clear in your own mind, you will be able to move into counseling with more confidence and sense of direction.

Six purposes are suggested here: (1) to help the couple understand the nature of marriage, interpreted, of course, in the light of the Christian faith; (2) to enable each partner to understand himself and what he brings to marriage as a person; (3) to guide the couple in being realistic about the adjustments they must make in marriage; (4) to assist them in discovering their strengths and weaknesses and what additional guidance and resources they need; (5) to stimulate meaningful communication between the two persons; and (6) to establish or strengthen a pastoral relationship with the couple.

These purposes are not separate items to be worked on one at a time. They are very closely interrelated and will overlap considerably in the process of being achieved. They are stated separately here for explanation and emphasis. Nor are they listed in the order of their importance; for establishing or strengthening a pastoral relationship with a couple is the primary purpose. Unless this is accomplished, very little can be done to achieve the other purposes.

The first two purposes are discussed in this chapter. A full chapter is devoted to each of the other four listed above.

Our overall aim is to give the couple—sometimes individually and sometimes as a couple—some specific help in their preparation for marriage. At the outset we should recognize that for most couples this help may be very limited. Indeed, many couples may not need, or desire, much more than a rather superficial review of some of the areas of concern mentioned here. But we need to recognize that each of these areas is important and should be given some attention with most couples. We should be prepared to explore in depth one or more of the following areas with a few couples.

Begin Where They Are

In helping two persons understand the nature of marriage the pastor must begin where they are in their understandings. But he will have in mind certain concepts that he considers essential to a Christian interpretation of marriage. He also has some responsibilities to himself as the one who must decide whether or not to marry a particular couple.

To begin where they are, it may be necessary to start with the *wedding* rather than with marriage. The couple may come wanting to prepare for the wedding—an event—rather than for their relationship. They may have many questions about the rehearsal or the reception as well as the ceremony itself. Some churches have developed a policy statement covering questions about decorations, music, picture-taking, and so forth, so as to protect and enhance the worshipful nature of the service.

In the back of *To Love and to Cherish*, the manual for engaged couples, you will find a Wedding Information blank which will help get at these questions.

In any case, we must begin with the couple's immediate concerns. Their questions need to be handled with care. For, if their questions are brushed aside, the couple may feel that the minister does not care about *them* either. One of the primary aims of the initial interview is to establish a relationship of warmth and trust which will facilitate free and open sharing.

Review Understandings

As soon as the couple is ready, you will want to help them review their understanding of the nature of marriage and guide them in evaluating this in the light of the Christian faith. (In the previous chapter "Toward A Theology of Marriage," you will find some background material that may be helpful to you at this point.) You may want to explore the couples' understanding of marriage in relation to the concepts of monogamy, vocation, covenant relationship, and other elements of a Christian marriage.

The first of these concepts is our belief that *marriage is a lifelong union of one man and one woman based on love and loyalty.* Do both partners understand that the vows say "so long as you both shall live"? Do they really intend their marriage to last "till death us do part"?

Do they know what it means to "forsake all other" and "keep only unto him (or her)"? Most couples respond rather quickly to this, saying that this means sexual fidelity. But very few relate it to the scriptural account in Genesis 2:24: "Therefore a man leaves his father and his mother and cleaves to his wife, and they become one flesh." They may need some help in shifting their primary loyalty from their family of origin (especially their parents) to the new union they are establishing.

Do they understand that both love and fidelity are essential foundations of marriage? Does their understanding of love include a positive attitude toward sex? These and other questions may help clarify their understanding of the nature of marriage.

The term *Christian vocation* applied to marriage may be new to most couples. But they are likely to know what is meant by entering marriage as a result of a deliberate choice in contrast to drifting into marriage. Most likely, however, they will need help in evaluating their decision in the light of God's will for them. How do they discover God's will? How do they know they are responding to his call to marriage?

Does the couple understand marriage as a *covenant relationship?* Are they prepared to fulfill each part of this commitment? Do they understand the significance of an unconditional covenant with each other before God? Do they realize that they are committing themselves not just to a lifelong union, but to a continuing effort to achieve a quality relationship?

Other elements which may be considered in connection with a Christian understanding of the nature of marriage involve at least five practical, yet deeply spiritual, concerns. One is the *personal commitment to God* as revealed in Jesus Christ. Another is the ability to give and receive *genuine love* in their relationship with each other. Ideally, this is a quality of self-giving love—sacrificing, forgiving, sustaining, affirming love.

A third concern is the importance of their *being a part of a Christian community,* being actively related to a church. A fourth is their *concern for others* which takes them beyond their own needs and satisfactions in marriage to involvement in service to the community and world.

The fifth concern is in the area of *purposes and values.* As a couple, how do they describe the overall goal of their life together? How is this related to God's will for them as they understand it? What do they believe is the highest value in this life? In what ways do they plan to help realize this value as a couple? What gives the deepest meaning to their marriage?

Readiness for Marriage

In his effort to help the couple understand the nature of marriage, the pastor also has some responsibility to himself. He must assess the couple's readiness for marriage to be sure he feels justified in marrying them.[1] This is both a matter of personal integrity—being true to himself as a minister of the gospel—and responsibility to the church and community, as well as to the couple. According to *The Book of Discipline of The United Methodist Church* (Par. 350.5) "the decision to perform a ceremony

---

[1] Charles William Stewart, *The Minister as Marriage Counselor* (Abingdon, 1961).

shall be the right and responsibility of the pastor." In the process he is helping the couple to "examine their total readiness for marriage." [2]

To meet this obligation he needs to ask himself some questions about the couple. Without being judgmental he can keep these questions in the back of his mind as he interviews the couple. Some of the questions will relate to facts; others will be based on his feelings about the couple. If he is doubtful about some of the answers he may require certain tests, request a series of interviews, or suggest a referral for additional help from another professional, such as a psychiatrist. After extending all the resources of the Christian faith to them, he may feel that he must refuse to marry some couples.

Questions to Consider

The following questions may help in the screening process:

Are some legal requirements being violated: license, age or consent of parents, health test, waiting period? Are any of your own church requirements being ignored?

Do these persons give frivolous reasons for wanting to get married?

Is one or both entering marriage under duress?

Are they so immature mentally and emotionally that they do not understand the meaning of the vows or give reasonable promise of fulfilling them?

Do they give indications that they do not intend to fulfill their marriage vows?

Are there any serious mental, emotional, physical, or other handicaps that might endanger their marriage? Have these been adequately understood, accepted, and dealt with insofar as possible?

Is there such marked personality incompatability that psychological testing is indicated?

Are there differences in age, background, values, and so forth, which will enrich or threaten their relationship?

If this is a second marriage, has sufficient time elapsed since the death or divorce for the person to have overcome the hurt and made adequate preparation for the new marriage?

[2] Rutledge, *Pre-marital Counseling*, pp. 18-19.

Is the couple willing to follow through with the premarital counseling interviews so that any questions may be checked out further or actually dealt with through counseling?

Just as a marriage counselor finds it necessary to evaluate a couple's ability to use counseling before proceeding too far into the process,[3] a pastor must assess a couple's readiness for marriage as understood within the Christian faith. Such evaluations can be only tentative at first and should be reviewed as the interviews progress. Clearly the pastor owes it to himself, the couple, and the community to be careful in deciding whom to marry.

Self-Understanding

Another major purpose of premarital counseling is to enable each person to understand himself and what he brings to marriage as a person.

Such understanding may be a growth experience for him. In counseling we attempt to help each person appreciate what he brings to marriage: his own style of life, his philosophy, attitudes and values; his temperament and personality characteristics, as these have developed out of his own unique experiences of family, religious, educational, social, and economic background.

In this whole area of self-understanding, a pastor must carefully weigh just how much it is possible to do with each person who comes to him for counseling. He must work within the limits of the person's readiness as well as the time available. What is presented here, therefore, is not what every pastor should attempt to accomplish with every person in premarital counseling. Instead it is a discussion of some aspects of our counseling with those few who evidence special needs and are willing to take the time to explore them in depth.

Undoubtedly the chief emphasis in premarital counseling is on the relationship between the persons who are getting married, for each one makes a unique contribution to the marriage in bringing himself to the relationship. Hence self-understanding is one of the major purposes of premarital counseling.

Premarital counseling *is not individual therapy*, but it does in-

[3] Dean Johnson, *Marriage Counseling: Theory and Practice,* Chapter 6, "The Beginning Interview," pp. 61-62, 72, 79-81.

volve helping persons achieve some measure of self-awareness of what he brings to marriage. Each pastor will have to decide just how far to go in this area with each individual. With some he may feel that almost no help is needed. He may feel that others should be referred for personal therapy. In either case, he should make such decisions on the basis of a careful evaluation.

The basic approach in this area, as in other areas of premarital counseling, is one in which the pastor assists the individual in discovering who he is and in developing a more adequate appreciation of himself as a person. The pastor does not size up the individual and tell him what he needs. When referral is indicated, however, it is the pastor's responsibility to recognize this need and try to help the person understand the value of the additional service. Certainly it is the individual himself who decides whether or not to accept the referral.

In helping an individual to understand himself as a person, there are two basic considerations, *identity* and *sexuality*, which underlie all others. Here are some issues and questions which may stimulate your thinking about the significance of these considerations in relation to marriage.

Identity

The ancient admonitions to "know thyself," "accept thyself," "by thyself" may seem like oversimplifications. But they get at something basic to healthy personality development, that is, self-understanding, self-acceptance, and being one's true self. To what extent does the individual in counseling with you evidence these qualities? Has he worked through the identity crisis? [4] Does he know who he is as a person? Does he have a clear understanding of himself as an individual in relation to others? Does he understand himself as a member of the groups out of which he comes? (This is why family, ethnic group, race, and nationality are significant.) Does he have a healthy acceptance of the background out of which he comes? What kind of accommodation is he making to various aspects of his background? Is he rejecting some elements? What is the meaning of these rejections? Does he have the inner

[4] Erik H. Erikson, *Childhood and Society* (W. W. Norton, 1964).

67

strength to work through these reformulations of his character? Is he growing stronger in this reshaping of himself, or is his ego strength being threatened or weakened by the struggle?

Self-esteem

How one feels about himself as a person is also of major importance. A strong self-respect and self-regard are important elements in an individual's psychic health. They are also important foundational elements in any wholesome relationship, especially the intimate relationship of marriage.

A person who has a low estimate of himself, who lacks a genuine self-love, will find it difficult, if not impossible, to love another person. Fortunately, most people coming to you will have a fairly mature sense of self-worth. A few, however, will need some help in discovering the causes for their self-depreciation. Some may grow considerably through experiencing full acceptance and affirmation in their relationship with you. Still others may need to be referred for more intensive counseling or therapy. (See pp. 89-91.)

When you do find a person who does not esteem himself very highly, you will want to check carefully on the partner too. What is it in the partner that causes him to be drawn to such a person?

At times the greater need for growth may be in the partner, who may give the outward appearance of being a fairly strong person, but who, within, is so unsure of himself that he needs a weaker person to be dependent on him. A marriage of such persons is likely to arrest or retard the growth potential in both partners. Such problems as these underscore the value of our having a psychiatric consultant on call whenever possible. Even though we may not need to call on him very often, it is reassuring to know that he is available when needed.

Sexuality

One aspect of being which is very important in self-understanding and in marriage is a person's feelings about his sexuality. This means the acceptance—preferably, the affirmation—of the fact that one is a sexual being, that one is a man or a woman and has sexual feelings.

To what extent has the individual accepted the fact that he is a sexual creature, that sex feelings are normal and wholesome? Is there any rejection of these feelings? Because of cultural conditioning, many persons come to marriage feeling that sex is dirty or "unladylike." Undoubtedly they need help in affirming sex as one of God's good gifts.

Others will need help in affirming their sexuality in the whole area of maleness and femaleness. This is not simply their gender, but the whole matter of what it means to be a man or a woman, and the healthy acceptance of masculinity and femininity—the feeling that "I'm glad I'm a man!" or, "It's great to be a woman!"

In exploring feelings about sexuality we may discover, for example, that a person has had some homosexual experiences. Some persons may be very much concerned about the effect of these experiences on their marriage. Some may be carrying an exaggerated feeling of guilt as the result of only one or two such contacts, which were a part of childhood or early adolescent sexual experimentation, and nothing more. A few, however, may be much more deeply troubled by an established pattern of continuing homosexual experiences, and may be questioning just who they are as sexual creatures.

Depending on our own attitudes and skills, we may be able to help those who have had only a few contacts. But persons in the latter group usually require more intensive and prolonged counseling or psychiatric help.

Use of the Premarital Questionnaires in the back of the couple's manual *To Love and to Cherish* is one way to open up some other specific areas of self-understanding. For example, see Questions 13, 31-33, and 38.

Philosophy of Life

An individual comes to marriage heavily loaded with intangible baggage. He brings his own philosophy of life, his own interpretation of certain moral and spiritual values, his particular attitudes toward people, issues, and institutions, his personal views on various political and social problems, his own commitments and involvements in supporting or challenging various aspects of our culture. These are some of the foundational elements of an individual's life and hence are basic to any deep and meaningful marriage relationship. If the pastor can help a couple clarify and verbalize some of these basic positions he may be making a fundamental contribution to a couple's future, not only to each individual's self-understanding, but also to the possibility of depth and growth in marriage.

Background

Each person also brings with him a variety of influences from the background out of which he comes. (Here again the Premarital Questionnaire will be helpful.) What kind of family did he grow up in? How did he get along with his parents and his brothers and sisters? How did they get along with one another? More important, how did this affect him? What is the present marital status of his parents?

In what kind of religious environment was he brought up? How active is he now? Why? How much education does he have? Is he still in school? Does he plan additional education? What kind of work did his father do? What is his own present occupation? Did his mother work outside the home? How did he feel about it? How much social life did he have during his teens? Since then? These are the kinds of questions that should help an individual to understand what kind of person he is and how his background has helped to make him what he is.

Personality

An individual needs to understand himself in terms of his temperament and other personal characteristics. In one way or another he may ask himself: What kind of person am I? How do I affect other people? Am I concerned mainly with my own needs and pleasures, or do I care about others? Am I outgoing and friendly, or reserved? Do I get angry easily? Do I express anger freely or hold it back? Am I rigid or flexible? Am I easily influenced by others? Easily depressed or discouraged? Jealous? Punctual? And so on.

Each person may be helped to understand himself better by having an opportunity to place himself somewhere on the continuum suggested by such questions as these: What kind of temperament do I have—controlled or impulsive? Aggressive or submissive? Warm or cold? Active or quiet? Serious-minded or lighthearted? Nervous or composed? Critical or appreciative of others? These are the kinds of traits the Taylor-Johnson Temperament Analysis attempts to measure.[5]

Interests

Still another avenue to self-understanding is by way of a summary of a person's interests and activities, such as various business and professional meetings, membership in certain clubs or organizations, specific hobbies, activities related to political or social concerns, creative activities, reading, social gatherings with friends, variety of outdoor activities, spectator or participative sports, attending plays or movies, and so forth. It is instructive to know not only the activities, but also the frequency and the enjoyment in each. (See Question 29, Premarital Questionnaire.)

Emotional Needs

Inevitably a person brings to marriage all his emotional needs—his personal and affectional needs, his need for companionship, his need to love and be loved. He brings his sexual needs and desires, which must be fitted into an ongoing pattern of mutually satisfying sex relationships; his sometimes ambivalent needs for itimacy and privacy. He brings his ego needs, especially his need for a sense of self-worth.

Under the pressure of so many depersonalizing forces in our society today, the search for satisfaction of these personal needs in marriage may place heavy demands on a partner and create severe strain in the marriage relationship. On the other hand, finding mutual satisfaction of these needs in marriage can strengthen the relationship and give both partners a sense of well-being.

Motivations

Through premarital counseling it may be appropriate for you to help some persons explore the motivations they bring to marriage.

[5] See Charles William Stewart, *The Minister as Marriage Counselor*, for a brief discussion of the use of tests.

Some of these may grow out of significant relationships unsatisfied or distorted during childhood. Marriage may be an effort to satisfy some of these basic needs, however belatedly.

In counseling, many partners may discover some motivations that led them to choose each other on the basis of complementary self-fulfillment. It is as though one discovers in the other that part of himself which is as yet unrealized. For some couples this intermeshing of their personalities works as smoothly as hand-in-glove. For others, it creates a great deal of friction. This complementarity may be healthy or unhealthy, and may call for additional professional help.

Growth and Change

Everyone, unless severely crippled psychologically and spiritually, brings to marriage the potential of growth. For there is within each person a God-given drive toward health and wholeness. People can change; and they can change for the better, even though this may be difficult. They are most likely to change when they feel that the person trying to help them really cares and is capable of giving them the assistance they need.

Self-understanding, in itself, is one form of growth. At the same time it lays the foundation for future growth.

Perhaps we should emphasize again, however, that premarital counseling is not intended to be solely, or even primarily, a search for self-understanding. But one of our aims is to help two persons realize and assess what it is they bring to the marriage relationship. For the quality of that relationship will depend largely on what the individuals bring to it.

CHAPTER 5

Adjustments and Role Expectations

One of our aims in premarital counseling is to guide the couple in being realistic about the adjustments they will have to make in marriage. Many couples do not realize that they are adjusting to marriage itself as well as to each other. But most of them do have some knowledge, however sketchy and incomplete, about some of the areas of adjustment, such as sex, finances, or family. Our purpose is to make sure they are not overlooking any significant area of adjustment. We are also concerned that they be realistic in their expectations regarding their roles as husband and wife.

One way to check on possible adjustments is the use of the Premarital Questionnaire in the back of the couple's manual *To Love and to Cherish*. In fact, the questions have been devised for this purpose. See especially Question 38 on disagreements. Of course other areas of agreement or disagreement may be revealed in almost every other question by comparing the responses. (See "Use Questionnaires," begining on p. 147.)

Unrealistic Expectations

Some couples approach marriage with totally unrealistic expectations. Their dreams of marriage are indeed romantic and illusory, unreal fantasies of impossible anticipation. In spite of much evidence to the contrary, many still look upon marriage as a magic potion to cure all of their problems.

Stimulated by our culture that is highly individualistic and pleasure-seeking, is it any wonder that so many persons think first of their own happiness and what they can get out of marriage, rather than about the other person or the effort a good marriage requires?

Some persons are unrealistic not only in what they expect but in how they expect it to happen—almost automatically, without any effort on their part. This expectation is fostered by the fact that many young people today have so much done for them, so much given to them. They feel that if they love each other, all they have to do is let it happen! Fortunately, this applies to a relatively small number, but still enough to require our special attention. It also applies to a lesser degree to a much larger number. Often these couples are not totally unrealistic, but unrealistic about only one or two areas of adjustment.

Overly "Realistic"

On the other hand, there is an increasing number of young adults who go almost to the opposite extreme. These are the ones who have become disenchanted with anything that has a hint of the sentimental about it. They are so "realistic" about the business of marriage that they give very little place to feeling. They are so sophisticated that they are never swept off their feet by anything, especially not by love. They appear to be calm about almost everything.

These persons are careful about advance planning. They have everything under control. In fact, they may be so careful with their money that they cannot enjoy splurging on a date. Or money may be unimportant to them, something to be used. These are the ones who want to be so successful in business that they do all the right things for the organization. They go through all the proper motions, but without much spirit.

74

Both the unrealistic and the overly realistic persons are likely to resist premarital counseling, the former because they are afraid that talking about their relationship will somehow diminish their happiness, the latter because they think they do not need it—they know what they are doing. Both kinds of persons need to experience pastoral concern for their welfare and have the opportunity to test it.

The vast majority of young people are somewhere between these extremes. To be sure, most of them still approach marriage somewhat starry-eyed and floating on Cloud Nine. There is nothing wrong with stars and clouds—so long as they do not interfere with responsible handling of the realities of marriage. In fact, one of the aims of premarital counseling is to enhance the thrill and excitement of getting married and to encourage the continuation of genuine romance in marriage. We do not want to dull the spirit, but to throw around it the framework that will conserve and release it. A good counselor is not one who takes the joy out of preparing for marriage, but one who gives the kind of assistance that increases the joy of it.

Inadequate Preparation

One reason why most couples approach marriage unrealistically is that they come to it without adequate preparation. In one sense everything that happens to a person from birth is preparing him for marriage. But some of these experiences are hurtful and may make it difficult for him to achieve the mutually satisfying adjustments required by marriage. At best this is a hit-and-miss kind of preparation, with no organization, and sometimes little depth.

Each young person comes to marriage having been exposed to particular husband-and-wife roles, and each partner's experience may be quite different. They may feel that these roles have been appropriate for their parents, but may not be suitable for young couples living in today's changing world.

In spite of the fact that many schools and churches are making special efforts at better preparation for marriage, particularly at the high school level, the majority of young people still come to marriage with inadequate preparation. This leaves the door open for the kind of preparation that can be done through premarital counseling. Even though the opportunity comes very late to most pastors they can still do much to help many couples. In fact, the pre-marriage period is viewed by some as one of the most "teachable moments" in a person's life.[1]

Adjusting to Marriage

One of our primary aims in premarital counseling, then, is to help couples realize what it means to adjust to marriage as a new state in life, as well as to each other. One area where marriage calls for changes is the area of freedom and responsibility. When two persons are married they are exchanging the freedom to act as unattached individuals for a different kind of freedom with each other. Previously each has been able to make his own decisions almost without reference to anyone else. Now, in marriage, the partner is involved in almost every decision. After the wedding almost every move must be considered in terms of how one's husband or wife feels about it, or how it might affect their life together. Likewise marriage is a relationship that carries a great deal of responsibility with it. Although each of the partners is still an individual, responsible for his own life to a large degree, each is responsible for the other. This is illustrated in the marriage vows when each promises the other "to have and to hold, from this day forward, for better, for worse, for richer, for poorer, in sickness and in health, to love and to cherish. . . ."

Marriage means a new way of life, a new set of values and goals. It means obligations and responsibilities, as well as pleasures and privileges. Many people approaching marriage do not realize the extent of these changes and need help from their pastor to face them.

Adjusting to Each Other

Since marriage is such an intimate and inclusive relationship, helping a man and a woman adjust to each other as *two whole*

---

[1] "Here is one of the 'teachable moments' or opportunities for learning, the like of which comes only a few times after early childhood. With the total impetus of nature, tremendous growth can occur, if motivation is stimulated and direction is provided. A minimum of concentrated help here can bring about personality changes which might take years of psychotherapy to effect later." Aaron L. Rutledge, *Pre-marital Counseling*, p. 7.

persons is one of the most significant services of premarital counseling. The establishment of a mutually satisfying relationship with each other is basic to the ability of each to adjust in other specific areas, such as sex or finances.

It is inevitable that some tensions, and even open conflicts, will develop when two unique individuals come together in marriage. No matter how many interests and values they hold in common, they are bound to have differences too. Basically, of course, this is because one is a man and the other is a woman. Maybe this sounds like a simple matter of physical sex differences. But there is also the whole matter of sexuality as maleness and femaleness. And this includes their being persons as well as the roles they perform. (See pp. 151-52 for "A Marriage Role Expectation Inventory.")

In spite of much talk today about the disappearance of sexual distinctions—and much of this is happening—the fact remains that marriage partners are still a man and a woman, each with a personal approach to life. The present-day transition and confusion in sex roles creates real problems for some couples—problems of uncertainty, threat, conflict. Other couples make a continuing effort to understand what is happening to them and work together creatively to develop a mutually satisfying relationship.

Dynamic Interaction

This adjustment of two persons in marriage involves the relating of all aspects of their personhood, as outlined in the above section on self-understanding. This includes the total dynamic interacting of two whole persons. Each partner meets the other with his own particular constellation of attitudes toward himself and his sexuality, his philosophy of life and system of values, the influence from the various aspects of his background, his interests and activities, and individual personality characteristics and emotional needs.

A couple may need guidance in evaluating their own special way of interacting. Are they in basic agreement (or conflict) regarding their philosophy of life? Do they share similar value systems? At what points do they differ? How serious or superficial are these

77

differences? Is similarity or difference in various aspects of their background—family, education, economic, social, religious—such that their relationship will be enriched or endangered? Do they have many interests in common? Do they enjoy doing the same things? To what extent is each person learning to share in the other's interests and activities?

Most emphasis, however, is usually focused on personality characteristics and emotional needs in trying to determine *compatibility*.[2] How does each partner react to the temperament or disposition of the other? How do their personality characteristics relate? Do they clash or harmonize? Are they able to meet each other's emotional needs? If serious differences are evident, psychological testing may be indicated.[3]

Special attention may be given to the complementary theory of mate selection,[4] mentioned briefly above. Often the very need that brings a couple together—finding fulfillment in the other—may be the thing that creates friction between them.

For example, a serious-minded woman and a light-hearted man may be drawn to each other. Each needs the complementary quality of the other. When such needs mesh harmoniously, they are compatible. But this combination may be the source of conflict, especially if the woman feels that the man is not serious enough to be the head of the house, or if he feels that she is expecting too much of him. Actually conflict here is between their temperament needs and their role expectations.

Adjustments in Certain Areas

Probably the most frequently used approach in helping couples to be realistic about the adjustments in marriage is concentration on certain areas of their relationship. Usually selected are religion, money, common interests and goals, sex, work, and in-laws.

[2] See Blood, *Marriage.*
[3] See Stewart, *The Minister as Marriage Counselor,* for a brief discussion of the use of tests.
[4] See Harold T. Christensen, *Handbook of Marriage and the Family,* pp. 665-70; for full discussion, see Robert F. Winch, *Mate Selection;* for criticism, see Henry A. Bowman *Marriage for Moderns,* pp. 5-7; for this and other theories of mate selection, see Paul Landis, *Making the Most of Marirage,* pp. 264-66.

Approximately three-fourths or more of United Methodist pastors indicate that they usually discuss these subjects with couples. Here are fourteen most frequently mentioned subjects listed in order of frequency and with percentages:[5]

Subject	Percent
Spiritual significance of marriage	90
Religious faith of the couple	89
Meaning of the marriage ceremony	85
Money matters	80
Common interests and goals	78
Sexual relationships	75
Occupations, wife working	75
Relationships with relatives	74
Where they will live	71
Birth control and family planning	64
Desire for children by both	63
Dynamic emotional forces	55
Family backgrounds	49
Relationships with old friends	33

It is interesting to speculate as to why certain subjects are discussed much less frequently than others; for example, "dynamic emotional forces." Is it because we consider this area of a couple's relationship less important than religion, money, or sex? Or is it because we feel less qualified to work in this area?

Thirty percent of us indicated that "there are some subjects [we] feel deserve consideration," but we "do not feel qualified or comfortable in discussing with couples." When given the opportunity to indicate what subjects, more (15 percent) listed "sexual matters" than any other one subject. Only about 2 percent listed "dynamic emotional forces." [6] When we believe an area deserves consideration, but we feel unqualified to deal with it, doesn't this suggest either referral to other qualified professionals, or further professional growth on our part?

[5] Hill, "Premarital Counseling Practices," p. 77.
[6] *Ibid.*, p. 78.

Three areas of adjustment are given special attention here as illustrations rather than as a definitive coverage of all areas. Some pastors prefer the developmental task approach to be sure that a more comprehensive coverage is attempted. (See Chapter 14.) Others concentrate on marital role expectations.

Religion

The discussion of religion should include not only the spiritual significance of marriage and the meaning of the wedding ceremony (see p. 152) but also the religious faith of the couple—their beliefs and practices, their goals and purposes, their doubts and growing edges of faith. Often this discussion centers around the church or faith group they belong to and the extent of their activity. If they differ on religious issues they should discuss alternatives they are considering after marriage and how each one feels about the various possibilities. They may be helped to explore these in depth.

Devotional readings and Bible study in the home may be encouraged, often by the suggestion or gift of a book of daily devotions. More important, however, is a consideration of the moral and spiritual values they share (or differ on) and how they plan to express these in their daily living.

It may be difficult for many of us to keep from preaching a sermon at this point and to make the consideration of religion a true experience of enabling the couple to share their religious views and questions.

Money

Since money is mentioned most frequently as a cause of conflict in marriage, careful planning of finances should be encouraged. Of course in most middle-class marriages money problems are only the symptom of other conflicts. The real cause of conflict may be much deeper in the dynamic emotional factors of a couple's relationship. In some families, however, the lack of money is a root cause of problems and not a symptom. This is true in the case of many younger couples or of families from the culture of poverty or situations where employment is unstable.

Attitudes and feelings about money are most important and

should be explored in premarital counseling. Such exploration may uncover some surprising feelings, even for couples who think they have already agreed on how to handle their finances. It is important to get these feelings out in the open, where their meaning can be evaluated and the couple can work on them together. Some people consider money an end in itself; they may place a high premium on savings. Others may consider money as a means of making life more livable or enjoyable. Some consider it "mine" and "yours."

Pastors find that some couples need help in deciding on actual dollar amounts in their budgets, and may guide them in some reality testing. Pastors may help couples evaluate the usefulness of such practical suggestions as:

Seek mutual agreement on financial matters, with the partner best able to handle money serving as "treasurer of the corporation."

Have a joint checking account.

Buy at least minimum amounts of health and life insurance.

Seek out an experienced and trusted friend or relative to check with regarding any major purchases or investments.

When the wife works, use as much of her income as possible for major items, such as furniture or savings, and use the husband's income for ongoing living expenses. In this and other ways, plan ahead as to when wife should stop work (and income) to start a family.

Sex

In talking with a couple about their sexual adjustment the pastor may have three aims in mind: to provide the climate that will free them to talk about any sexual attitudes and practices that are important to them; to encourage a Christian attitude toward sex; and to make available specific guidance and resources in this area.

The Pastor's Attitude

The most important factor in providing the climate for the free discussion of sex is the pastor's attitude. This has more to do with his being the kind of person who is easy to talk with than it does with his adopting any particular approaches or techniques. This

81

means that the pastor must be a person who genuinely feels and expresses a helpful concern for the persons in counseling. This is a quality of being that obviates the possibility of a judgmental or condemning attitude. Such a pastor is not shocked, for example, by the report of premarital sexual practices—not because he is shielded by a thick coat of asbestos armor, but because his deep concern for the person affirms the personhood of the individual in spite of what he may have done.

Such a pastor does not probe into areas where he is unwanted. This is not because he guards himself against his desire to move in; but rather because he is sensitive in catching and reflecting the true attitudes that are only hinted at in words. By this approach the person feels understood and appreciated, and is freed to move into an examination of deeper feelings and to share any other disturbing experiences.

Those of us who feel uncomfortable in discussing certain sex matters should be careful not to exceed our limits. Otherwise, our own embarrassment or uncertainty may cause a couple to hesitate to dig into other areas at another time. It is wise for us to counsel within the limits of comfort. On the other hand, unless we go beyond these limits we may never enlarge the boundaries of our usefulness. Perhaps the best advice here is not "stop," but "proceed with caution."

The Individual's Attitude

Within a setting of acceptance the pastor will try to discern each person's attitudes. Then he will know just how much help is needed. He will encourage a positive Christian attitude, one which affirms and appreciates sex as a gift of God, to be enjoyed and not used only or primarily for procreation. The Christian view also sets sexual intercourse in the context of the total interpersonal relationship of two whole persons and does not treat it solely or primarily as a physical phenomenon. (See Chapter 3, especially pp. 50-51.)

We may expect a majority of persons we counsel—sometimes as high as three out of four—to need some help with attitudes toward sex. In spite of our freedom to talk about sex today, our past conditioning still hangs on in the form of negative attitudes, such as the belief that sex is either dirty or sinful, and is not enjoyed as much by women as men. Also the overemphasis on sex in our contemporary culture often fosters an exploitative attitude that is highly individualistic and self-centered pleasure-seeking rather than the kind of pleasure-giving that nourishes companionship. Fortunately such attitudes are improving. Most persons approaching marriage, however, need help from their pastor. Often the need for help is greater among middle-aged people than young adults. This is especially true when a person has felt used or abused in a previous marriage or in a premarital relationship. In such instances a series of individual appointments may be added to the usual pattern of interviews. Frequently the experience of discussing sex with the pastor in the setting of the Christian church has a very positive effect in correcting false information or in dispelling fears.

While many persons come to marriage with unrealistic expectations about sex, others actually have very limited knowledge and experience in this area. This is why pastors need to make available to all couples specific guidance and resources regarding the sex adjustment in marriage.

Some persons expect too much. Sex is so glamorized in our culture that some couples admit a letdown in the actual experience of intercourse. Some think that sex is the most important thing in marriage; others may expect a mutually satisfying experience (including simultaneous orgasm) on their wedding night or within the first week. When their expectations are not realized, they may be very upset, or feel inadequate, or suspect that there is something seriously wrong with them, or that they may be "incompatible." They need to know in advance that it takes time—often many weeks or several months—with a lot of give and take, for most couples to realize a good sexual relationship.

Some will expect a perfect sexual adjustment automatically, without any special knowledge or skill or effort on their part. They come to marriage thinking they know all they need to know, when actually their knowledge and experience are quite limited.

In this area of sex adjustment some pastors feel that they should limit their premarital counseling to a discussion of attitudes. For various reasons they feel that they should not make any references to anatomy or give any guidance in the techniques of sex relations. Most pastors, however, do give their couples one or more books on marriage, such as the couple's manual *To Love and to Cherish*, which has a chapter on sex. In addition, many pastors make available to most of the couples a book on sex. (See suggestions on p. 155.)

Most pastors in our church (61 percent) refer a couple to an agency or another professional person for additional guidance in connection with their premarital counseling.[7] Most of these referrals are to a family service or other counseling agency or to a medical doctor. It is likely that much of this counseling is related to the sexual adjustment.

A small but growing number of ministers do give specific guidance in the sexual adjustment. They may point out some of the usual differences in the sexual responses of men and women, the value of having a medical doctor to check the hymen (as well as give a full medical examination and advice on birth control), the importance of clitoral stimulation, or suggestions for easing the tension some couples may experience in first intercourse. They may do this in response to the couple's request for information on the Premarital Questionnaire in the couple's manual, especially Question 34, or because of the implications of their answers to Questions 30 through 35. When an individual indicates a need for it, some pastors administer the Sex Knowledge Inventory (see description on pp. 163-65).

[7] Hill, "Premarital Counseling Practices," p. 68.

CHAPTER 6
Strengths and Weaknesses

Premarital counseling is an effort to assist a couple to discover strengths and weaknesses and to determine what additional guidance and resources are needed in further preparation for marriage.

For the couple, such discovery is a means of indentifying growth potential and enriching their relationship. It should also help them to discover areas of need and to assess their resources for meeting these needs.

For the pastor, counseling is an opportunity to direct one or both of the partners to whatever additional resources may be needed. This process also guides him in deciding when it is wise to give sound reassurance or other forms of support and encouragement. He does not overlook problems. But the emphasis is on what can be done to solve them and on facilitating growth and change.

Much of the preceding discussion related to self-understanding and adjustment may seem unduly slanted in the direction of individual problems or difficulties in adjustment between the partners. This is intentional, because the points at which there is a lack of understanding, an unrealistic expectation, or a problem of adjustment are precisely the points where counseling may be most helpful to most couples. For other couples, however, a more positive kind of preparation may be more appropriate. The emphasis in the following pages is intended as positive rather than negative and is aimed at helping the couple discover and capitalize on their strengths.

Discovering Needs

First, some additional attention must be given to needs which have not yet been mentioned, or which have been referred to only briefly. The pastor must be alert to any physical, emotional, or intellectual difficulties that might overburden the marriage. Does either partner have any physical handicaps or limitations? Are both in good health? The answer to this last question, of course, calls for a general health examination by a medical doctor.

Premarital Medical Examination

It is strongly recommended that, whenever possible, each pastor require all couples to see a physician, preferably one experienced in premarital counseling.[1] Thirty-seven states require some kind of health examination in preparation for marriage, in addition to the traditional blood test. But many of these examinations are inadequate, and most of them cover much less than is here recommended. Such a premarital consultation with a medical doctor should include a general health examination, examination and consultation for sexual adjustment, and contraceptive information and prescription.

[1] Books recommended for the physician are: Rutledge, *Pre-marital Counseling* (*especially* Chapter 8, "The Physician's Role in Preparation for Marriage"); Abraham Stone and Lena Levine, *The Premarital Consultation, A Manual for Physicians* (Grune and Stratton, 1956); Mary S. Calderone, *Manual of Contraceptive Practice* (Williams & Wilkins, 1963); Richard H. Klemer, *Counseling in Marital and Sexual Problems* (Williams & Wilkins, 1965); Ethel M. Nash, Lucie Jessner, and Wilfred Abse, eds., *Marriage Counseling in Medical Practice* (University of North Carolina Press, 1964); and Joseph B. Trainer, *The Physiologic Foundations for Marriage Counseling* (Mosby, 1965).

The first purpose of the premarital medical examination is to evaluate the general health of both the man and the woman. This examination usually is related to their physical fitness for parenthood as well. This may not seem very important at the time of marriage, especially when a couple plans to wait two or three years before having their first child.

One such couple found themselves with an unplanned pregnancy soon after marriage. The wife died in labor on her first wedding anniversary. The doctors who were called in said death was due partly to the fact that the baby was deformed and stillborn, and partly to lack of adequate medical care earlier. This recommendation for a premarital examination is not made out of fear that many couples will suffer a similar tragedy. One is too many. It is made out of the knowledge that couples need the information, guidance, and assurance that only a medical doctor can give.

The second purpose of the premarital medical examination is to check on the couple's readiness for sexual adjustment. This is important for both the man and the woman.

The man may have questions and anxieties that call for the doctor's guidance in understanding his wife's sexual needs, and in initiating intercourse.

A part of the woman's vaginal examination will be an examination of the hymen, to find out if it needs dilating in preparation for intercourse. Many women will need no medical aid. But if dilation is indicated, it is usually accomplished artifically rather easily, or it may require a simple surgical procedure. Ordinarily this can be done in the doctor's office with only a local anesthetic. Some women today still insist that defloration be done only by the husband in intercourse. A medical examination will indicate whether such procedure is safe. Frequently the hymen is so tough that entering marriage without medical help is risking too much suffering and placing too great a strain on the marital relationship.

This proved to be the case with one couple who came to a church counseling center for help with their sexual adjustment. They had been married six years and had two children. But they had never had a satisfying sex relationship and the wife had never had an orgasm. In trying to discover the origin of their difficulty the pastoral counselor learned that complete intercourse was not possible for the first two years of marriage. The tough membrane made it impossible to penetrate the hymen. It was only after the hymen was ruptured during the birth of their first child that the vaginal orifice was enlarged enough to permit normal intercourse.

The counselor wondered how the couple had been able to endure the nervous tension caused by this condition during their first two years of marriage. He discovered that, fortunately, their overall relationship was strong enough to tolerate the sexual frustration.

We may wonder that anyone would be hesitant to accept the medical aid that is readily available today, but some people still need the pastor's insistence that the medical examination be a routine part of premarital counseling.

A third reason for the premarital medical consultation is to obtain information about family planning and birth control. More and more communities are developing planned-parenthood clinics to render this service under competent medical supervision. Of course it is not absolutely necessary to get such information or materials from a physician. Some contraceptives are readily available in most drug stores. But following the direction of a doctor or a clinic is the safest and best way to do family planning.

Many wives will want to work for a few years after marriage while their husbands are in school or getting started on a job. So they will need to wait for a time before starting a family. In such cases, only medically approved methods of contraception should be used, and these only under a physician's supervision. Because of possible side effects, the Pill should be used only by women who are under their doctor's care.

Some couples will also want information about the RH factor, and still others may need help in facilitating conception.

Qualified Physicians

Physicians qualified to give this kind of help, however, are hard to find. One study found that only 37 percent of the doctors interviewed "routinely made suggestions to premarital patients about contraceptive methods, whereas twenty-eight percent included contraceptive infomation only if it was specifically requested by the patient." [2] The figures only relate to contraceptive advice, for even fewer physicians offer "counsel concerning sexual and marital adjustment." More than 55 percent of the doctors reported that "nothing in their medical school education had prepared them for helping patients with marital adjustments," while more than 66 percent "reported negatively in this respect about their internship and residency training." [3]

It is obvious that not every doctor is equipped to offer the kind of premarital consultation recommended here. Thus, it may do little good simply to tell a couple to see their family doctor. It may be necessary to give them the names of two or more physicians who are known for this kind of counseling. In most communities a pastor will have to visit the physicians personally to find out just what their practice is regarding the premarital consultation, and to find ways he and the physician can work together for the good of the couple.

If no qualified physician is available in the immediate community, perhaps one can be found within fifty or seventy-five miles to whom couples can be referred. Some couples may complain about such distances, but most of them drive farther than that to a football or basketball game!

Other Referrals

Are there any intellectual or emotional difficulties that might overburden the marriage? Does the premarital interview raise enough questions in the pastor's mind to indicate that intelligence or psychological testing is needed? If so, these tests require the services of a trained psychologist. Most of us simply do not have the training that equips us to do this kind of work. Although giving some of the paper-and-pencil tests seems simple enough, interpreting them is another matter.

In most cases it will be best to delay further counseling until any necessary testing and interpretation are completed. Even then it may be necessary to refer some persons to a psychiatrist or to a social work agency or mental health clinic where a psychiatric con-

---

[2] Calderone, *Manual of Contraceptive Practice*, pp. 96-103, for study of North Carolina reported by Ethel M. Nash.
[3] *Ibid.*

sultant is available. Each pastor should know all such resources available in his community, or nearby, so he can make direct referrals when the need is indicated.[4]

Referral is a delicate matter. It should be handled in such a sensitive manner that the person realizes the pastor does it out of genuine caring for him. Referral is a procedure which the person must come to see as having real value for him—value enough for him to accept it positively and make good use of it.

Referrals may be needed in a variety of other areas, such as legal, financial, and household management. Legal questions may be as simple as asking requirements for obtaining a marriage license, which every pastor should know. Or questions may be more complicated than he can handle, such as those related to property and alimony involvements carried over from a previous marriage, or grown children trying to prevent their aged father from changing his will in anticipation of a new marriage. Obviously it is unwise for the pastor to do any guesswork here. He should be prepared to refer whenever necessary.

The pastor may be able to help a couple set up a budget and to advise them regarding a joint checking account, but he may find it best to have a concerned banker or home economist to do this part of his counseling regularly. At times some couples may also need the services of a loan officer or someone who can help them do some long-range planning in refinancing their school debts in order to be able to get married. Some couples may have money available for investment and need expert advice. Others may need the guidance of the county welfare department, especially where aid-to-dependent-children grants are being made for children from a former alliance, whether legal or common-law marriage, or no marriage at all. If a man (or woman) needs retraining for a new job before he can afford to get married, he may find help available from the state vocational rehabilitation office.

For help in household management, the services of a home economist may be of great value. Many family service agencies offer this kind of help along with other kinds of counseling,

⁴ William B. Oglesby, *Referral in Pastoral Counseling.*

including a rather full plan of premarital interviews. Counseling is usually a part of the service of planned-parenthood clinics also.

Services available are so many and so varied that each pastor needs to know which are available in his community and to make good use of them. Most state mental health agencies (or similar groups) have directories of such services, free or for sale at very small cost.

Reading

In checking a couple's strong and weak points in marriage preparation the pastor is likely to find that most of them could benefit from further reading and study, either as individuals or as a couple. In addition to the manual *To Love and to Cherish*, which is strongly recommended as a gift to each couple at the very beginning of counseling, most couples will need to do some additional reading. (See suggestions on pp. 154-55.)

Mixed Marriages

Some couples will need books on special subjects, such as interfaith marriage.[5] Perhaps the best book for a Protestant who is considering marriage with a Roman Catholic is *If You Marry Outside Your Faith*, by James A. Pike.[6]

There is a great deal of talk about changes in the Roman Catholic position on this subject. At the time of this writing, however, this expectation of change is more anticipation than actualization. For there has been no change in the basic position of the Roman Catholic Church on this subject, or on its stand on birth control.

Actually, there are only two slight modifications in their position on interfaith marriage. One is that in some sections of the country the pledge to bring up children in the Roman Catholic Church may be made orally instead of in writing. But the word is expected to be just as binding as the signed statement. The other change is

[5] For help with the whole area of mixed marriage, see Henry A. Bowman, *Marriage for Moderns*, Chapter 6; Judson T. and Mary G. Landis, *Building A Successful Marriage*, Chapter 13; and Paul H. Landis, *Making the Most of Marriage*, Third Edition; Albert I. Gordon, *Intermarriage: Interfaith, Interracial, Interethnic*.

[6] Harper & Row, 1962.

that a Protestant minister may now say a prayer of blessing for the couple at a wedding in the Catholic Church, *after* the couple has been pronounced married by the priest.

Another book on interfaith marriage may be helpful to couples who have already decided to be married. It is *Protestant-Catholic Marriages Can Succeed*, by Paul and Jeanne Simon,[7] written by a fairly mature couple out of their successful experience in an interfaith marriage.

A few pastors have used films in connection with their premarital counseling. One on Protestant-Catholic marriage which might be used is *One Love, Conflicting Faiths* (TRAFCO). Originally intended for group use, this film also has value in stimulating a couple to discuss several areas which need to be considered in interfaith marriage.

The pastor needs to guide the couple in exploring their motivations for marriage, especially when a mixed marriage is being considered. This will require more time than is allowed in the four or five interviews suggested as the basic minimum in this manual.

In many—perhaps most—mixed marriages a couple may be drawn together by genuine love and a sense of basic similarity in values and interests which transcend their differences and are truly much more important to them. Such couples need their pastor's help in realistically facing tensions their differences may create within marriage as well as any difficulties with others outside their marriage. But they also deserve his support in facing necessary adjustments, and his reassurance when he discovers their strengths.

Some other couples, however, may be driven to marriage by rebellion against their parents or against social pressures to "marry your own kind." This rebellion may be a deeply neurotic desire to punish their parents. Some marry outside their ethnic group because they feel rejected by their own group. Others may marry out of a desire to accelerate social reform, as is believed to be the case in some interracial and interethnic marriages today. Still others marry out of a sense of adventure, in response to the glamor of the

[7] Association Press, 1967.

mysterious in a person from a different origin or background. Some intercultural marriages occur simply because of the proximity of two people at the age of marriage. This is often true in time of war or military occupation. The man may have a girl waiting at home, but the one available at the moment may be chosen.

Another reason for some mixed marriages is the expectation of personal, social, or economic gain as, for example, when one "marries up" for personal gain of one kind or another. Or a man who does not like the present equalitarian relationship between men and women in the United States may seek marriage with a woman from another culture who has been trained to look up to men. She may make him feel superior.[8]

The pastor sometimes discovers that motivations for marriage are unsound. Then he may feel that he must recommend that the couple postpone their wedding, perhaps to allow for additional counseling. If they are unwilling to postpone, he may feel that he must go ahead and marry them.

On occasion, after the pastor has helped a couple to question the soundness of their motivations, they will agree to postpone their marriage, and later may break off their relationship altogether. Their motives, whatever they may be, should be explored so that they may be understood, and perhaps changed, or strengthened. In any case, the couple will then be able to make their decision on the basis of deeper understanding.

Discovering Strengths

As the pastor helps couples discover the strengths and weaknesses they bring to marriage, he may be surprised to find that they have more strengths than weaknesses. The reason for his surprise is understandable. Most other pastoral counseling is problem-centered: a person with a problem he cannot handle alone comes to his pastor for help. The pastor, if he is not careful, may allow himself to become so absorbed in the problem-centered approach that even in premarital counseling he sees only the difficulties.

[8] Blood, *Marriage.*

Preoccupation with problems poses real dangers. One is the probability of giving couples the negative impression that we are always looking for problems and are unable to see their strong points. This may cause them to resist counseling or to misuse it. Premarital counseling must deal with any problems that need attention, of course. But it must also help couples develop their strong points, strengthen and improve some of the positive growing edges of their relationship. To the extent that it is really appropriate, premarital counseling should put just as much emphasis on the strengths of a couple as on their weaknesses. We should not hesitate to call attention to, and to explore, their strengths in a positive, affirming manner.

When he is alert to the strengths a couple brings to marriage, the pastor may be impressed by three qualities that are often overlooked—their desire for preparation, their potentiality for growth and change, and their determination to succeed in marriage.

Open to Help

Many couples will be open to receiving all the help they can get, not because they approach marriage with a great deal of fear or uncertainty, or are overloaded with problems, but because they realize that marriage is an important and sometimes difficult undertaking. They appreciate all the help their pastor can give them. This may sound strange to many of us, for we are still struggling with the problem of getting couples to come to us in time for premarital counseling. Yet this appreciative attitude is being expressed by more and more couples today, as they discover the values in such counseling.

Potential for Growth

We must realize, of course, that a couple does not have to be perfect to insure a sound marriage. If so, there never would be any satisfying marriages! For we are all imperfect human beings. Accepting this fact of life has real value. It keeps one from expecting too much of himself and permits him to be more understanding of his partner.

But this is not the kind of acceptance that means idle resignation. In a very real sense this is accepting one's shortcomings as a challenge to change and improve. Most persons are endowed with an ability to grow and to change for the better. They have a God-given inner drive toward wholeness that responds to intelligent direction. This potentiality for growth is one of the greatest strengths a couple brings to marriage. It makes helpful counseling possible.

Determination to Succeed

Many authorities feel that a couple's greatest strength is the determination to make their marriage work. Expressed positively, this is the drive to succeed; expressed negatively, it is an unwillingness to give up, or to consider divorce as a way out.

That is, two persons are determined to do their best to get the most out of their marriage. And this is one of the powerful forces for enrichment in marriage, and ought to be supported and encouraged.

When to Give Encouragement

What are some other strengths we should be alert to recognize? What should be encouraged? At what points is reassurance warranted?

In trying to answer these questions it is essential that we do not gloss over problems. This does not mean that we should so emphasize one of two minor points that we minimize areas of serious need. We must not give the false reassurance that says, in the face of a difficult problem, "Oh, don't worry about that; you won't have any trouble working that out when it comes along"—particularly when there is no ground for such a statement. Instead, we must be sensitive to basic foundational strong points that can be built upon, that can serve as the center around which new growth and greater strength can be developed. This is beginning with reality and enriching it.

Many couples coming to their pastor to be married will show an adequate understanding of the nature of marriage. Perhaps they have carefully evaluated their love to be sure it is true love, and they plan to be faithful to each other. Many of them will not be rushing into marriage blindly, but they have been very careful in making the decisions regarding their engagement of several months and in setting the date for the wedding. Some of them will be very serious about their marriage as a sacred commitment to each other in a covenant relationship. They may be sure they are entering a lifelong union.

The sensitive pastor will pick up such important understandings and will try to help enlarge their meanings for the couple. For example, he will explore with the couple ways in which they may enrich their understanding of love and fidelity and will help them appreciate some dimensions they may not have been aware of before, such as enlarging the meaning of fidelity to include much more than faithfulness in sex relations.

Here is another example of how a pastor may work with a couple to help them discover areas for growth, rooted in their already sound understandings. Both persons may be dedicated Christians, and may be actively related to the church. The pastor might ask how their faith affects their marriage. Through free question-and-answer discussion they may come to see more clearly the value of Christian character in marriage. They may give some evidence of being able to give and receive love, but questioning may reveal that they need to give more attention to the forgiving aspects of love. Discussion may bring out the fact that they are actually searching for guidance in readjusting as a married pair to some of the fellowship and service activities they have been previously related to. They may be afraid of being cut off from old groups, and uncertain about new ones open to them. They may want their life together to be based on concern for others as they express it through their work—she as a nurse and he as a teacher, for example.

Perhaps after sharing some of the positive values and meanings of their work, a couple may be ready for some exploration of how their concerns for others can reach beyond persons they serve directly in face-to-face situations.

The above is not meant to suggest a subtle manipulation of couples into preconceived patterns, but is an example of how recognized strong points may serve as the basis for further discussion that may result in deeper enrichment or wider horizons.

Most of us are quick to respond with deep feeling for a person who is struggling with a problem, for we are aware of his need for our concern to support him while he is working it through. Some of us, however, may not be as ready to respond to a fairly mature person, because we think he does not need us. We must remember that the fullest enrichment and growth of a mature person may also be stimulated by the expression of genuine encouragement.

Self-understanding

In his premarital counseling, the pastor is justified in giving support and encouragement to a person entering marriage when the person demonstrates an understanding of himself: when he knows who he is and shows mature judgment and intelligence in practical affairs; when he evidences a healthy affirmation of his sexuality (although he may need some fuller understanding of sex relations); when he understands fairly well what he brings to marriage in terms of his philosophy and system of values, various aspects of his background, personal characteristics, interests, and activities; and when he is reasonably healthy emotionally.

Reassurance and Support

What is again recommended here is the judicious use of reassurance and support to stimulate further growth for both the individuals and for their relationship. Many couples will be fairly realistic about the adjustments they will be making in marriage. They may have reasonably high expectations of each other and of marriage. But these are in line with their abilites. Neither person expects the other to be perfect. Instead they accept their immaturities, but have a healthy desire to change, to grow, and to improve. They know they will have to work at their marriage. They are aware of certain differences, tensions, and conflicts and are realistic in expecting some of these to continue after marriage. They already have some experience in working through conflict in several areas. They give evidence of communicating with each other at some depth. They indicate some skill in problem-solving.

Many couples will realize that they are adjusting to marriage as well as to each other. Their personalities may be complementary and compatible. They may enjoy many common interests and activities, but also grant each other the freedom to be an individual.

97

Even before they come to premarital counseling, many couples will have evaluated specific areas of their adjustment, such as religion, sex, money, and their relationship with relatives. They may be active in a church, although not always in the same church. Their income may be adequate, and they may be planning a sensible budget and household-management procedures. They may express warm feelings for each other and have healthy attitudes regarding sex. Some couples will give indications that they are being sensible about preparing for most of the developmental tasks they will face after marriage. Most couples will also have a strong positive feeling about their marriage and will be entering it with a feeling of security and a sense of belonging to each other.

All in all, the pastor may have a very good feeling about a couple's readiness for marriage. If he does, there is no reason why he should not share his feeling with the couple. This kind of genuine reassurance may relieve some of the tension they are bound to feel and stimulate them to continue to grow in their relationship.

Chapter 7
Communication

One of the major purposes in premarital counseling is to facilitate and improve communication between the partners, and to assist them in increasing their skills in problem-solving. We want to help them both to understand the meaning of genuine communication and to actually experience it in their dynamic interaction.

This means that premarital counseling either begins or improves the process of deeper sharing that is expected to continue and improve in marriage. We also want to help the couple discover the value of problem-solving and increase their skills by actually applying them to specific areas of their relationship when there is conflict or an issue to be resolved.

A Two-Way Process

What do we mean by communication? Communication is the open, dynamic interaction of two (or more) persons involving some kind of message and response, usually conveying both feelings and ideas, which may be expressed in actions as well as words.

In premarital counseling the pastor tries to help a couple understand and experience the fact that communication is a two-way process. It is not a matter of one person "telling" the other something, to which he may pay almost no attention. Unless someone is listening—really listening and reacting to what is being said—the message is not getting through. Of course, the reacting may occur in silence. It does not have to be expressed openly. It may be happening in the mind of the listener. But this is a response. Communication, then, is not monologue but dialogue. Both a sender and a receiver of a message are necessary.

Much of the time, however, one person does not hear what is actually said. He hears only his own interpretation of the message. He hears what the message means to him. Is it any wonder then that the message which gets through is so often very different from the one intended? It is important that the receiver try to understand what the message means to the sender. It is also essential for the sender to try to be clear in the signals he sends.

In all communication, but especially in marriage, it is essential for the receiver not only to get the message but to respond appropriately. For couples, this means being sensitive to each other's needs and responding to those needs. If one is either unwilling or unable to "hear" the other's needs or to respond to them, their relationship will suffer.

Persons can learn to be more sensitive listeners and more appropriate responders. They can also learn to communicate better. Premarital counseling offers an opportunity for such learning.

Ideas and Feelings

The message in communication usually conveys ideas and feelings, both important in the content of communication. But frequently the intellectual concept is emphasized, while the emotional content is almost completely overlooked or ignored. Many couples make the mistake of trying to interact with each other on the rational level and forget the feelings.

To illustrate: A young wife came home from work and complained to her husband, "The boss really messed up things for me at the office today. You remember he let me handle the correspondence on that Randall account? Well, today, without saying a word to me about it, he just dictated another letter changing the specifications I sent to them yesterday."

To which the husband replied, "Well, he's the boss. That's his job." And then he wondered why she stormed out with "Oh, men!"

What the husband said was true. He stated a fact, on the rational level; but he missed the emotional meaning of what his wife had said. If he had been more perceptive of the feeling content in what she said, he might have replied, "Yeah, it's pretty tough being pushed aside and contradicted." On receiving this kind of sensitive response, instead of storming out she might have shed a few tears, with a sense of release from the tension she had been carrying all day and probably with a feeling of warmth for a husband who understood.

The pastor can assist couples in being more sensitive to each other's feelings. He can guide them in finding ways of helping each other express their true feelings. He can help them see that both their positive and negative feelings need to be brought out into the open so they can be understood and handled constructively by the two of them. He can point out the danger in feelings being hidden. Hidden, they are likely to cause additional hurt; suppressed, they are likely to fester and worsen. They may cause the individual more inner uneasiness and may also damage his relationship with another person, perhaps without his realizing what is causing the trouble.

Words and Actions

Communication may take the form of actions as well as words. Some couples make the mistake of thinking that they are communicating only when they are talking to each other. To be sure, words are important, but behavior—gestures, facial expressions, mannerisms, posture, even silence as well as specific acts—may convey much more meaning than words, or at least with more force. A slammed door, for example, communicates anger more effectively than words do.

The pastor can help a couple see that behavior is a language, and can help them learn how to interpret the meaning of their behavior. The pastor can also help couples see that there is danger

101

in playing down the importance of words. They need to know that it is essential for them to take time to talk things over. If they keep on saying "Not now, we'll talk about that later," they may find so much unfinished business piling up that they are never quite able to catch up. And their relationship may suffer.

Open Communication Essential

Why is communication so important? Real communication is not simply what happens *between* a couple, as though the process were something outside each one, something suspended between them. Rather it is the dynamic involvement of two persons in each other's lives. This kind of communication is an absolute necessity in marriage.

Some kind of communication is essential to the psychic health and growth of the individual. The maintenance of life depends on a person's being able to communicate the message of his own selfhood to another and being able to receive a similar message from another in response. Emotional starvation can result if a person does not receive this kind of communication. Without the ability to communicate, an individual would become completely isolated from others, and his very personhood would atrophy.

Free and spontaneous communication is also essential to the development of a depth relationship between two people. Thus they share each other's lives; a genuine sense of belonging develops between them; they feel secure with each other and have a sense of comfort and stability in their relationship. A deep and open communication between a man and a woman makes possible the enrichment of their relationship through a sharing of their sufferings and struggles, their values and aspirations.

Developing open communication through premarital counseling is especially important, because couples usually have some negative conditioning to overcome. Certainly modest progress can be made with some, but the barriers to open communication are often deep, and require extended help.

Most persons have been trained not to express certain feelings or interests. They learn to hide behind masks, so that it is very difficult for one person to get to know another. Perhaps because of unpleasant, or even traumatic, experiences, many learn to protect themselves from further possibilities of hurt. Hence they close down certain lines of communication.

Even in marriage some couples find that they are constantly hurting each other because they are not fully or accurately communicating. So they close off one area after another, out of supposedly positive consideration for each other, until there is very little open relationship left to them. Some authorities believe that lack of communication is the chief source of difficulty in 85 percent of unhappy marriages.

In premarital counseling the pastor can help couples see the importance of communication in their developing relationship, for marriage is an intimate relationship that must be nourished to grow. Genuine communication is one way to do this. Since marriage is a dynamic, ever-changing relationship, constant interaction between the partners is required. Without communication two people would remain two private, isolated individuals. Marriage is an achievement which requires the cooperation of both husband and wife. Inevitably, tensions and disagreements will arise in the normal course of living. These must be faced and worked out together—through communication.

Improving Communication

How can the pastor help a couple to improve communication? There is some value in helping them discover some of the barriers to communication in their experiences with each other. They may discover that they are too busy to talk things over, much as they need to or want to. This may be true especially of a couple in the rush of the last few days before the wedding.

One person may complain that the other does not listen when he is talking, or does not take seriously what is being said. The other may respond negatively to small talk and retreat from communication because he feels nothing important is happening. Being all wrapped up in personal interests and concerns can also block communication. This personal preoccupation may vary from a temporary concentration on one's own affairs to a thoroughgoing self-centeredness.

Even though it is necessary to express real feelings to communicate in depth, emotions can also block communication.

These include guilt feelings, feelings of inferiority, of hostility or resentment, or of simple fatigue. The couple should be helped to see, for example, that there are times when it is best to postpone working on a problem until they "feel better." Some couples will discover that they have little to talk about, because they are divided by different interests and values.

Overcoming Barriers

It might be helpful, also, for the pastor to guide the couple in evaluating ways of overcoming any barriers to communication that they discover in their relationship. They may come to realize that real communication does take time and effort, and cannot be achieved on the run. They may have to control their schedule so it allows them more time together. One person may discover that he must make a continuing effort to listen. He may have to try hard to "be there 100 percent" instead of letting his mind wander off on his own concerns. This may suggest that one partner will need to become more interested in the activities and concerns of the other.

Some couples may discover that one or both of them have some deep negative feelings which they need to work through with their pastor or other counselor. They may find that any improvement in communication lies in an individual's becoming the kind of person who is easy to talk with. Others may find that they need more sharing of values and interests so as to develop more common goals and activities. Still other couples may decide that one person needs more freedom to develop personal interests in order to have something significant to share when they do have time together.

Counseling Stimulates Communication

Perhaps the best way to stimulate communication between two persons is to let it happen naturally in the process of premarital counseling.

The very fact that the couple has agreed to come for counseling may start them talking about the seriousness of their marriage. Or communication may be stimulated by one of them (usually the woman) accepting the pastor's invitation to the first interview, even though the other is questioning the value of counseling. She may have to do quite a bit of communicating to get her fiancé to agree to come in, and they may discuss a number of concerns that are pretty important to her in the process. This may happen entirely outside the counseling sessions.

In the sessions themselves some issues or concerns may be brought out into the open, which the couple may have been avoiding in an effort to keep down conflict. They may begin to talk over some of these with the pastor, but will continue their conversations on their own. The pastor may sense an area of need and open it up for this purpose. Or there may be some topics they have already talked about, but only superficially, and then pushed aside, thinking they had covered the subject. The pastor can encourage them to pursue these in greater depth simply by asking a few questions that have some meaning for them.

When the pastor reads the wedding ritual to a couple and they begin to discuss certain points, communication may be initiated that will continue long after the session is over. During the joint interview, one partner may notice the other's reaction to a particular statement or question. He may not say anything about it at the time, but later may inquire about its meaning, and a whole flow of conversation may follow.

Private Appointments

In addition, the pastor has an opportunity for stimulating deeper communication in the appointment(s) with each person alone. For example, there may be an issue which should be faced by the couple but, for one reason or another, they hesitate to get into it. In the confidentiality of the private appointment one partner may muster enough courage to bring it up.

This is exactly what happened in one session with a man alone. The pastor, reflecting on the young man's feeling that he did not expect to have any "trouble" after marriage, went on to ask, "If you could imagine yourself having some disagreement after marriage, what do you think it might be about?"

The young man hesitated for a long time, obviously searching. Finally he answered, "It might be over her father. I think she feels too close to him."

So they took time to explore the meaning of these feelings for the new relationship. This particular young man gained enough strength in premarital counseling to discuss the father-daughter relationship with his partner, and discovered that it was not as much of a problem as he had feared. He later shared with his pastor his conclusion that without the stimulus of the question he might never have brought his fear out into the open and discussed it, and might have been overly sensitive about it for years to come.

This is the kind of fear that one person might hesitate to bring up with his partner present. Most engaged persons are very careful not to criticize each other's families, especially the parents, and especially not within a few weeks of the wedding! Thus the private appointment can stimulate communication, not only between the individual and the pastor, but also between the partners themselves.

Premarital Questionnaires

One of the most effective ways of stimulating communication is through use of the Premarital Questionnaires in the back of the couple's manual *To Love and to Cherish*. (See detailed instructions for use of the questionnaires, beginning on p. 147.) Each person, as he fills out the questionnaire, will probably find questions about many items he had not previously considered important. Now he begins to wonder, "If these are important enough to be on the form, I guess they are important enough for us to discuss." Thus, couples begin to talk about new subjects.

Or partners, as each fills out his own questionnaire, become curious as to what kind of answer the other gave to a particular question. One may ask, "How did you answer Number 30 about affection?" and "Why do you feel that way?" And, of course, a new line of communication is initiated.

Even though the pastor instructs each person to fill out the questionnaire alone, he may tell couples that as soon as they have completed the form they may talk about any of the questions. In fact, he should encourage them to do so.

Communication may also be stimulated by the way the pastor uses the forms. In comparing the man's answers with those of the woman, he may discover some interesting differences. In the

106

private appointment and without violating the confidence of either person, the pastor can explore reasons for their answers.

The reading the pastor asks the couple to do may also initiate deeper communication. For various reasons the woman usually takes more time for reading. She may then try to share with her partner some of the information she has gained.

The pastor may ask a couple to read a book together. Or he may suggest that they read certain chapters on particular subjects, thus encouraging extended conversation on particular topics. The pastor may bring some of the reading into the conversation during the interviews and suggest further homework for the couple. A few couples take time to read aloud portions of one or more books and then talk about them. Reading aloud together a devotional book such as Snyder's *Inscape* or David Mace's *Whom God Hath Joined* may encourage a couple to have further conversation in some very significant areas of their relationship in the light of the Christian faith.

Problem-Solving

A crucial dimension of communication is decision making and problem-solving. In premarital counseling sessions a pastor can assist couples in developing the ability to make decisions together and to solve problems as they come along. He can encourage a couple to take an optimistic attitude toward their marriage, so that they expect the best from each other without expecting too much. At the same time, he can help them to be realistic in anticipating disagreements and to be prepared to cope with disagreements as they arise. Expectation of some differences will help a couple resist panic when they have their first quarrel. They will not feel that their marriage is destroyed by one argument. The pastor can also emphasize that even conflict, when handled properly, can become a powerful motivation for improving their marriage.

Facing Conflict

By facing constructively any conflict that arises during the counseling session, the pastor can help a couple experience the benefits of such an encounter.

The premarital-counseling film for ministers and physicians, *Before They Say I Do,* has one scene of conflict. John and Sally are in the middle of their second joint interview with their pastor. John has just expressed a rather strong feeling about money. They will have to make some sacrifices until he "can get a better job," he says.

Sally volunteers, "We can always get money from my dad."

The pastor asks Sally how John feels about that. She seems surprised at the question, but says she does not know.

The pastor turns to John and asks, "How do you feel about that, John?"

He replies with deep emotion, "I wouldn't like it!" He raises his voice, "In fact, I wouldn't like it at all!"

Can you put yourself in that pastor's place? What would you do after this outburst? More important, how would you feel while it was happening? What effect do you think your feelings would have on Sally? On John? What would you do next? Would you do or say anything at this point? What? Why?

Perhaps most of us feel uncomfortable in the presence of conflict. We may have been sensitized to the damages of conflict by having to deal with strong differences of opinion and disagreements that have arisen in board meetings or committees. We may even have lost a few church members because of some conflict situations. In various ways most of us have been conditioned to avoid conflict or to try to reconcile those in disagreement. After all, we are called to a "ministry of reconciliation." Would you try to reconcile Sally and John at this point?

When conflicts such as Sally and John experienced do come out, the couple needs to feel our support. At this point we are not concerned about the eventual outcome. We are supporting them in the process of confronting an issue that needs to be explored at the feeling level. It is far more helpful, of course, for them to experience an accepting attitude from us. In addition, it may be important for us to give some verbal reassurance to back up our attitude, and to clarify in their minds what we really mean. This kind of attitude and verbal reassurance can help to head off any guilt feelings that might follow such an outburst—guilt feelings that might cause either person to withdraw. It can also clear the way for further exploration of the issue, and can aid in getting at the roots of the conflict. This means that we must avoid taking sides with, or blaming, one or both persons. Instead we help them center on, and explore the meaning of, the issue which gave rise to the strong feelings. This may be the beginning point for them in learning some of the steps to follow in problem-solving.

Basic Steps

There are five basic steps in problem-solving: (1) define the problem; (2) gather data; (3) explore alternatives; (4) choose one alternative and act on it; and (5) evaluate the results.[1]

When related to marriage problems, Steps Three and Four as listed above had best be expanded, as will be explained. Normally these steps are followed in order, but not necessarily. For example, a couple may discover that the process of gathering data about the causes of a conflict creates in itself enough understanding to make going through the other steps unnecessary. On the other hand, in the process of exploring alternatives, they may discover another, more urgent problem and decide to double back immediately to Step One to work on it.

Here are these basic steps in problem-solving, briefly described, as they may be followed in the counseling session or by the couple on their own:

1. *Define the problem.* This may be much more difficult than it seems at first, and that may be why some people say that "defining the problem is half the solution." Many couples will find it hard to admit that they have a problem. They may need help in facing it squarely for what it is. Together a couple should try to put into words just what the problem is so they can agree on what it is they are working on. If it is not a "mutually defined" problem, they may be moving in opposite directions. One of the major tasks of the pastor in this kind of situation is to help the couple center on the problem and attack it instead of each other.

2. *Gather data.* Next they need to get all the pertinent information about the problem that is necessary. They should list all the possible causes they can think of. This may be a very painful process for some. Together they should try to figure out what led

---

[1] For a good discussion of the process, see Tom McGinnis, *Your First Year of Marriage*, Chapter 4, "Developing Ways of Reaching Decisions and Settling Disagreements."

up to the problem, and what brings it to a head just now. General-ly, the more details they are able to get on the origin and develop-ment of the problem, the better they will be able to understand it. Again the pastor may assist the couple in directing their energies to the causes of the problem rather than blaming each other. He can also help them to be sure that they are getting at the roots of their problem and digging them out, instead of only chopping off the problem at the surface and leaving the roots to produce more problems in the future.

3. *Explore alternatives.* This step is a whole process in itself. Before actually listing the various alternatives for action, the cou-ple should set some goals. The emphasis should now be placed on the positive side. What is it they want to accomplish together? The pastor may need to encourage them to do some dreaming about what they would like to have in their marriage in the place of the difficulty that has arisen. The pastor will also check to be sure they are being realistic about the possibilities they consider. He will want to be sure they are choosing their purposes together. For if one does all the choosing, and the other only tags along, neither will have very strong motivation for working toward a solu-tion.

Next, the pastor may aid the couple in gathering all the in-formation and insights available regarding possible solutions. Do they need to do some reading? Perhaps the pastor can recommend certain books, or chapters in books, that will help. Do they need information or guidance from other people who have been through similar situations? Do they need to see other professionals for knowledge or insights? Again the pastor will want to be sure the couple is moving along together at the knowledge level, so far as is possible.

The pastor may guide each person in trying to put himself in the other's place. Each should try to find out how the other really feels about the problem and its possible solutions. Is there anything holding the other person back from expressing his opin-ion or sharing his real feelings? What can be done to free him to express himself freely and frankly?

Then the pastor may assist in actually listing all possible alter-natives. What can the couple do about the problem, to move in the direction of solution? What can the persons do separately? What can they do together? How does each person feel about each of the alternatives? Which alternatives promise some real help? Is the couple moving toward the goals agreed upon?

4. *Choose one alternative and act on it.* This is the point at which the pastor can help a couple to evaluate each of the possible alternatives in the process of narrowing down the list to one course of action. To do this he must make sure the couple examines the positive and negative aspects of each alternative. What does each alternative have going for it? What forces might block it? At this point he must be sure the couple checks each alternative against their goals to make certain it has a good chance of accomplishing the purpose desired.

Now the couple is ready to decide which seems to be the best course of action. They will also need to determine exactly what is to be done. Who does what? Do they need help from others? The pastor may need to support them in the decision and the action, but the couple should actually put their plan into practice. They should try it out.

5. *Evaluate the results.* Actually evaluation should take place at every step in the process as the partners ask each other, "How are you doing?" The pastor will be asking himself: What is happening to them—these persons—in the process? What is happening to their relationship? Are they becoming more mature persons in the process? Will what they are learning from working their problem through help them in the future?

The pastor may also have additional questions. If the problem is not solved or the issue is not resolved, is it wise for the couple to repeat the problem-solving process? Or is this a condition or situation they must continue to cope with without an immediate solution? How much more can they do on their own, or do they need additional professional help to discover new insights about themselves or their situation before moving further in problem-solving?

When to Seek Help

Finally, the pastor may need to help couples evaluate their effectiveness in problem-solving on their own, and recognize when they need to seek outside, perhaps professional, help. Here are some simple guidelines.

Couples need help (1) when they are unable to agree that a problem exists, yet one is very upset about it while the other is not concerned; (2) when they both agree they "have a problem" but are unable to define it; (3) when they try to go through the steps of problem-solving but never seem to get anywhere; (4) whenever communication breaks down and they simply cannot talk about the problem (a clear signal to call in help!); (5) if their efforts to improve their relationship only make matters worse.

CHAPTER 8
The Pastoral Relationship

The final major purpose of premarital counseling is to establish or strengthen a pastoral relationship with the couple. Although listed last, this might be considered the primary purpose of premarital counseling. Establishing a strong pastoral relationship may be the most important result of counseling for the couple, especially if they should need to return for marriage counseling.

What is meant here is much broader than the counseling relationship itself, although this is part of it. We are thinking of a pastoral relationship that extends far beyond the counseling session. For some couples, this relationship may have been established before the premarital interviews. If so, premarital counseling should deepen it, as suggested on pp. 38-43. If there has been no deep relationship before, it may begin in counseling.

Dynamic Interaction

This relationship is a dynamic interacting of two (or more) persons, in this case the pastor and one person or the pastor and the couple. In premarital counseling the relationship grows out of the sharing of feelings and attitudes, the suffering and struggles, or the joys and aspirations of one or both of the engaged persons with their pastor, who respects, accepts, cares about, and affirms them as persons of infinite worth.

In some respects this relationship is like a bridge joining two islands. Contrary to John Donne, each man is, in a real sense, an island of private consciousness, which can be shared with another only as bridges of understanding are built between them.

The relationship may be initiated by either the pastor or the person. If an individual or a couple is aware of a problem that calls for counseling, they may make the first contact by asking for help. Usually, however, the pastor initiates the relationship by asking the couple to come for counseling. Either one may reach out to the other, but for a relationship to be established the other must make a response. Without both the reaching-out and the responding there is no relating, no real meeting of persons.

To have any dependable stability the relationship must be anchored deep within the being of each person. A superficial anchorage at either end makes for a flimsy relationship, which may break down at any time. The amount of traffic or weight it can carry depends on both the anchorage and the strength (or quality) of the relationship.

A Strong Relationship

What is it that gives quality to this relationship? What can the pastor *be* and *do* that will inspire the kind of response that will aid the personal growth and enrich the marriage of a couple? The suggestions which follow are not neat categories, but perspectives on the helping relationship, each very much interrelated with all the others. Each is a facet of the whole relationship.

Love for Persons

The pastor can love, for love leads to trust. When he truly cares about, and really wants to help the persons he counsels, a genuine warmth and concern is communicated. Unless a person has been so severely hurt in other relationships that he has been forced to "close up" in order to protect himself, he is likely to respond

114

positively, even though cautiously. He may move toward the pastor slowly, checking out the relationship to see "what is in it for him." He may respond by testing more than by trusting at first. As he discovers that the pastor's concern is genuine, that the pastor really is dependable, he is likely to become more open and willing to share. In short, he may become more trusting and may really work at building a strong relationship.

Respect for Persons

The pastor can respect the persons he is counseling, for respect encourages responsibility. When he shows respect for an individual as a person, that individual may be freed to discover inner resources and to take more responsibility for himself or for his relationship in marriage. Especially is this true when the pastor expresses his respect by trusting the individual to make his own decisions, or by recognizing him as a free agent responsible for himself. The person is helped to stand on his own feet rather than made to be dependent on the pastor, but he is given freedom to fail.

The pastor does not attempt to do too much for him; he is allowed to move at his own pace. The pastor does not threaten him by probing into areas where he is not wanted, but respects his privacy, and goes only as far as the person is ready to move at the moment. The pastor keeps confidences, for he respects a person for himself, and never as an object to be used for another's purpose.

Acceptance of Persons

The pastor can accept, and acceptance enhances understanding. When a person is accepted as he is, he may be encouraged to share more of his inner self, and in the process may gain more insight into himself. Or as a couple learn that their relationship is accepted for what it is, they may share more of their deeper feelings about it and hence gain a better understanding of what it means to them. Instead of any kind of rejection, the person, or the couple, and their relationship are accepted as they are.

In this accepting spirit, then, the pastor listens not only to the words but primarily to the heartbeat and tries to reflect the feel-

115

ings that may be hidden between the words. If the pastor is sensitive enough to reflect these feelings accurately, the person is likely to feel, "He does understand me!"

A genuine desire to understand, with repeated efforts to clarify, has about the same positive effect as actually understanding. When a person feels accepted and understood he can drop some of his defenses, which have been consuming so much of his energy. Then he can put that energy into learning to understand himself and into improving his relationship with his future partner.

Affirmation of Persons

The pastor can affirm, for affirmation stimulates growth. As helpful as acceptance is, the sensitive pastor knows that it does not go far enough. Therefore, he appreciates and affirms the person as a child of God. Instead of judging, condemning, or correcting an individual, the pastor appreciates him as a person in the process of becoming, as one appreciates and enjoys a sunset unfolding its beauty. This positive affirmation of personhood sustains an individual in a supportive relationship when it is needed. This kind of affirmation helps to give a person a sense of self-confidence, a genuine self-esteem so essential to his ability to love another. It also inspires and challenges a person to become his best possible self under God, and to give of himself to another.

A Helping Relationship

The pastoral relationship is a helping relationship. Out of his rich experience in counseling, Carl Rogers suggests a series of ten questions we might ask ourselves in seeking to create a helping relationship both in premarital counseling and in our continuing pastoral care.

1. Can I be in some way which will be perceived by the other person as trustworthy, as dependable or consistent in some deep sense? I used to feel that if I fulfilled all the outer conditions of trustworthiness—keeping appointments, respecting the confidential nature of the interviews, etc.—this condition would be fufilled. But experience drove home the fact that to act consistently acceptant, for

116

example, if in fact I was feeling annoyed or skeptical or some other non-acceptant feeling, was certain in the long run to be perceived as inconsistent or untrustworthy. I have come to recognize that being trustworthy does not demand that I be rigidly consistent but that I be dependably real. . . .

2. Can I be expressive enough as a person that what I am will be communicated unambiguously? When I am experiencing an attitude of annoyance toward another person but am unaware of it, then my communication contains contradictory messages. My words are giving one message, but I am also in subtle ways communicating the annoyance I feel and this confuses the other person and makes him distrustful, though he too may be unaware of what is causing the difficulty. . . .

3. Can I let myself experience positive attitudes toward this other person—attitudes of warmth, caring, liking, interest, respect? It is not easy. I find in myself, and feel that I often see in others, a certain amount of fear of these feelings. We are afraid that if we let ourselves freely experience these positive feelings toward another we may be trapped by them. They may lead to demands on us or we may be disappointed in our trust, and these outcomes we fear. So as a reaction we tend to build up distance between ourselves and others—aloofness, a "professional" attitude, an impersonal relationship. . . .

4. Can I be strong enough as a person to be separate from the other? Can I be a sturdy respecter of my own feelings, my own needs, as well as his? Can I own and, if need be, express my own feelings as something belonging to me and separate from his feelings? When I can freely feel this strength of being a separate person, then I find that I can let myself go much more deeply in understanding and accepting him because I am not fearful of losing myself. . . .

5. Am I secure enough within myself to permit him his separateness? Can I permit him to be what he is—honest or deceitful, infantile or adult, despairing or overconfident? Can I give him the freedom to be? Or do I feel that he should follow my advice, or remain somewhat dependent on me, or mold himself after me? . . .

6. Can I let myself enter fully into the world of his feelings and personal meaning and see these as he does? Can I step into his private world so completely that I lose all desire to evaluate or judge it? There is a strong temptation to set students "straight," or to point out to a staff member the errors in his thinking. Yet when I can permit myself to understand in these situations it is mutually rewarding. . . .

7. Still another issue is whether I can be acceptant of each facet of

117

this other person which he presents to me. Can I receive him as he is? Can I communicate this attitude? Or can I only receive him conditionally, acceptant of some aspect of his feelings and silently or openly disapproving of other aspects? It has been my experience that when my attitude is conditional, then he cannot change or grow in respects in which I cannot fully receive him. . . .

8. Can I act with sufficient sensitivity in the relationship that my behavior will not be perceived as a threat? . . .

9. Can I free him from the threat of external evaluation? In almost every phase of our lives—at home, at school, at work—we find ourselves under the rewards and punishments of external judgments. "That's good"; "that's naughty." "That's worth an A"; "that's a failure." Such judgments are a part of our lives from infancy to old age. I believe they have a certain social usefulness to institutions and organizations such as schools and professions. Like everyone else I find myself all too often making such evaluations. But, in my experience, they do not make for personal growth and hence I do not believe that they are a part of a helping relationship. . . .

10. Can I meet this other individual as a person who is in the process of becoming, or will I be bound by his past and by my past? If I accept the other person as something fixed, already diagnosed and classified, already shaped by his past, then I am doing my part to confirm this limited hypothesis. If I accept him as in process of becoming, then I am doing what I can to confirm or make real his potentialities." [1]

A Goal Worth Pursuing

Establishing a pastoral relationship with a couple is a goal worth striving for, even if we should not be able to do much in achieving the other purposes of premarital counseling. With many couples, premarital counseling may be more like an annual medical checkup rather than problem-centered counseling. They may come to counseling with an adequate understanding of the nature of marriage, so the pastor is not able to make much of a contribution. He may not need to give much specific help either. Each partner may already know fairly well what he brings to marriage as a person. The couple may be reasonably realistic about the adjustments they will be making in marriage. They may be aware of their weak points

[1] Carl Rogers, On Becoming a Person (Houghton-Mifflin, 1961), pp. 50-55.

and be working on these. And they may be making good use of their strengths. The pastor may discover that they are already communicating with each other in depth and are using their skills in problem-solving. But if he does nothing more than establish a relationship with the couple, premarital counseling will be worth all the time and energy it takes.

Beyond what it does to facilitate the counseling process itself, why is establishing a pastoral relationship so significant?

When such a relationship has been established, the pastor is available if later pastoral care or marriage counseling is needed. To be sure, the pastor is supposed to be always available. But after an encounter in premarital counseling, he is emotionally more available. The doors are already open psychologically. The bridge is there to be used.

To some extent a good relationship may be carried over from one pastor to another. From a good experience in premarital counseling, couples may generalize that pastors care about persons and their marriages, and are capable of giving help. Unhappily, the opposite is also true. Pastors who do not take their premarital counseling seriously give the impression that pastors do not care, that they are inept in ministering to marital needs.

The effort to establish a pastoral relationship may have value even when a couple resists premarital counseling.[2] One pastor knew about a couple's approaching marriage several weeks before the wedding. But he was unable to get them to come in for counseling until he practically refused to perform the ceremony unless they did. They were both members of his church and residents of the neighborhood. At the pastor's insistence they came in very reluctantly the night before the wedding. The pastor did the best he could for them in the two-hour period they had.

He saw them together for about half an hour, going over the marriage ritual in an effort to help them understand the meaning of the vows they were about to take. The woman entered into the discussion as much as she could and tried to encourage the man to participate. But she was obviously embarrassed that he refused to comment except to answer yes or no to direct questions.

[2] Esther O. Fisher, *Help for Today's Troubled Marriages*, p. 195.

119

Then the pastor saw each of them alone for half an hour, the man first. But even in the private interview the man said very little more than in the opening session. The pastor admitted his own discomfort and tried to reflect what he thought the man was feeling in the strained situation, but to no avail. In her private session the woman talked a little more freely, but only superficially. The pastor was aware of a major problem but did not probe for it. She never brought it up.

The situation was not much improved in the last thirty-minute session with the couple together. Yes, they planned to be active in their new church after marriage. They wanted to start a family in a year or so, and she would see her doctor for birth control information. They thought they could handle their finances without any help from the pastor, thank you! And that was about it. To say the least, the pastor was very discouraged about these attempts at premarital counseling. He even wondered if it would have been better not to have insisted on going through the formality. But he had tried—perhaps too hard, he thought.

After the wedding the couple moved out of the city to a small town about fifty miles away, where the husband was principal of a small school. They came back home on holidays and attended church when there. But they had only casual contacts with the pastor for the next two years, mostly just speaking to him as they left the morning worship service.

After they had been married about two years, one day the husband called for an appointment for himself and his wife. Verbal communication had almost broken down between them, and they thought it might help if the pastor would see them. They came for appointments almost every Saturday for about three months, during which time they made considerable progress. As they came to the last session, it was the man who thanked the pastor and laughed about how different these sessions had been from premarital counseling. The pastor halfway apologized for forcing the premarital interviews. To which the man responded, "But you know, Pastor, I don't think I would have called you three months ago if you hadn't insisted on seeing us before we married."

PART III
Practice

CHAPTER 9

Educative Counseling

In this manual premarital counseling is understood from within the context of pastoral counseling as *a process in which a pastor helps one or more persons, or couples, or their families to review their readiness for marriage, to make plans, and to solve problems in the area of preparation for marriage.*[1]

This manual is concerned primarily with premarital counseling between a minister and a couple who are actually in the process of preparing for marriage and planning for the wedding which the minister will perform. It assumes that both the man and the woman are available for the counseling. At times, however, one of them may be unavailable, as when the man is in military service. Another exception is the engaged couple who may be evaluating their relationship and who decide not to marry.

On occasion, premarital counseling may include persons other than the couple. For example, parents of the couple may be a part

[1] Adapted from Charles William Stewart, *The Minister as Marriage Counselor.*

of the process when there are special problems such as premarital pregnancy, or when the couple is very young. At times certain individuals may seek out premarital counseling. A person who has no immediate plans for marriage may still want to know the meaning of marriage as a future possibility. Or a person who has been "jilted" may need help in adjusting to "no marriage." The pastor may also work with several couples in group premarital counseling.

Teaching and Counseling

The above definition of premarital counseling is an umbrella statement covering both the instructional aspects, called educative counseling,[2] and the person-initiated, problem-centered type of pastoral counseling.[3] In this chapter we explore some of the educative aspects of premarital counseling. In the next chapter we discuss problem-centered counseling.

For most pastors premarital counseling is an integration of both the teaching and the counseling functions of the minister. We call it premarital counseling instead of premarital instruction or premarital education because it is set within the counseling relationship.

The basic structure, content, and process of premarital counseling are derived primarily from the educative aspects of the process.

Structure

By structure we mean the overall framework of premarital sessions within which a pastor and a couple explore various areas of concern. To illustrate: A pastor may follow a basic pattern of four one-hour interviews. First he sees the couple together. In the next two interviews he has an individual appointment with each person. In the fourth they are together again. (For greater detail, see Chapters 11 to 14 on procedures and resources.) This pattern is called basic because it is the usual arrangement. But it may be

[2] See Howard J. Clinebell, Jr., *Basic Types of Pastoral Counseling*, Chapter 11.

[3] For an emphasis on the psychotherapeutic approach, see Aaron L. Rutledge, *Pre-marital Counseling*. Note, however, his recognition of the appropriateness of both types of counseling, pp. 58-63.

changed by adding other sessions whenever an individual or a couple need more counseling than this pattern calls for.

The first interview is structured to establish a free and open relationship—a primary counseling goal—as soon as possible. In most situations this is also the time to take care of certain items of information regarding the wedding plans. (See the Wedding Information forms in the back of the couple's manual *To Love and to Cherish*.) Primarily, however, the purpose of this first session is to explore with the couple their understanding of the nature of marriage and the meaning of the vows they are assuming, and to try to determine where they are in their preparation for marriage. These goals are basically educational in nature.

The private interviews are structured around the concerns the couple brings to marriage as persons—their personality, background, values, and so forth—and probably some of the areas of adjustment that are easier to talk about in private than in joint sessions, such as compatibility, sex, or in-laws. Again, these are content areas.

In the final joint interview the pastor and the couple may discuss certain developmental tasks or plans for adjustment in marriage, such as planning for children, earning and spending their money, developing a common philosophy or religion. These areas of concern are content areas and hence educational in nature.

Flexibility

It should be emphasized that such a structure must be flexible in order to give more attention to issues or concerns where there is greater need, or to exclude altogether areas where there is little or no need. This structure must also be flexible at the point of permitting the basic framework of interviews to be changed at any time, whenever a problem emerges that calls for further counseling. Such a problem and the counseling called for may be handled in the regular interview time; or one or more additional appointments may be needed, for the individual alone or for the couple.

Many pastors find it difficult to know when they are doing educative counseling and when they are functioning in problem-centered counseling, since premarital counseling is such a mix of the two. Actually premarital counseling is an integration of the two, or it continually shifts from one to the other. A clear understanding of both kinds of premarital counseling should help us function more skillfully in each and, therefore, be of more help to a couple.

Some pastors make the mistake of trying to conduct all joint interviews as educative counseling and all private appointments as problem-centered counseling. They may run into real difficulty when a problem arises in the joint interview that calls for further counseling, or in the private appointment if no problems are evident.

Usually the private interview is mostly instructional; for example, the pastor responds to the questionnaire request for sex information by explaining the nature of the reactions of the opposite sex or giving suggestions about first intercourse. On the other hand, in the middle of a joint interview the process may change. The pastor may be talking with a couple about the importance of seeing a physician for their premarital medical consultation and may sense a sudden embarrassment and reticence in them to talk about it. Without probing, the pastor may reflect their feeling that the subject is difficult to talk about. The couple may feel enough understanding and support from him to tell him that they think the woman is pregnant. Suddenly the situation shifts from educative to problem-centered counseling.

Sensitivity

To respond to this kind of situation the pastor must be sensitive as well as flexible. He must be sensitive to a need whenever it arises. This does not mean that he is forever suspicious, always expecting something to happen and therefore always probing for problems. But it does mean that he must be keenly aware of any change of feelings whenever the atmosphere becomes charged with emotion or when one person gives the other a negative signal of any kind. He must never be so preoccupied with his own (educative) agenda that he is unaware of what is going on between the couple.

Similarly, whenever a problem arises, he must be ready to shift roles immediately. Again he must not be so obsessed with his agenda that he cannot drop it and move with the couple to their chief concern at the moment.

Content

In its educative aspects, premarital counseling has a content —something previously experienced or understood by others which may be shared with or made available to a couple. This content includes not only information, experience, and skills, but also principles, values, and beliefs. Some of this content may be recorded in books, films, tests, and so forth. It may also be in the mind and experience of either the pastor or the persons he counsels, something they have learned (facts, skills) or have committed themselves to (values, beliefs).

The basic body of this content is suggested in Part II, Purpose and Content, and in Chapter 3, "Toward a Theology of Marriage." The word "suggested" is used advisedly, for the content is outlined only briefly in this manual. For a fuller coverage of the recorded content, refer to the books listed in the Bibliography. A wise pastor never tries to review the entire content with any one couple. They do not want to know that much about it. And it would take more than a year to do it. The pastor is very *selective* in his use of content, matching available knowledge to the *needs* of the person or couple.[4]

Even in its educative aspects, premarital counseling is much more than information-giving, although this is an important part of the process. A pastor should never hesitate to give information when this is needed. The most common procedure in this aspect of premarital counseling is for the pastor to stimulate conversation with the couple by asking questions. These questions must be non-threatening, yet reveal the present state of the couple's preparation and readiness for marriage. What is recommended here is not probing, for probing is questioning into the inner world of the person and usually revolves around thoughts, attitudes, or experiences which he does not wish to reveal to others. This questioning is a process in which the pastor takes the initiative, but he does

[4] See Clinebell, *Basic Types of Pastoral Counseling*, pp. 191-93.

not hesitate to yield that initiative to one or both of the individuals when they are ready to move into other areas of concern.

Process

The educative part of premarital counseling is characterized by a process in which the pastor functions in a way different from that used in problem-centered counseling. This process involves four steps.

Review Readiness

As educative counseling, premarital counseling is a process in which a pastor helps persons or couples review their readiness for marriage. In this review the pastor guides them in both an exploration and evaluation of their understanding of the nature of marriage, their knowledge of what they bring to marriage as persons, the adjustments they are making with each other as they prepare for marriage, and their plans for making their adjustments (or achieving their developmental tasks) after marriage.

Identify Needs

In the midst of this review the pastor assists persons or couples to identify and assess their needs related to preparation for marriage. These include not only their immediate needs as individuals or as couples in their present relationship while preparing for marriage, but also their anticipated needs in the adjustments they will have to make in marriage. They may be aware of some of these needs, such as understanding how to adjust sexually or how to manage their money. They may be able to identify these rather easily through responding to a few questions, either verbally or in writing. (See pp. 147-51 for an explanation of the use of the Premarital Questionnaire in the couple's manual.) But they may not be aware of other needs which the pastor has in mind, such as the need for an understanding and acceptance of marriage as a covenant relationship.

In assessing needs, the pastor and the couple together will choose to work on certain ones in the counseling process itself and leave others to the couple to do with them what they want to or can do on their own. They will carefully weigh the relative

126

seriousness of each need. The couple may want to work on those areas which seem most urgent to them at the moment. In this sorting process, however, the pastor will need to guide the couple in balancing the urgency of certain needs with their ability to use available information, values, and so forth.

Discover Resources

Next the pastor helps the couple discover methods and resources to meet these needs. Much of this will be done in conversation as he meets with them individually and together. If, for example, their need is for deeper communication in certain areas of disagreement, the pastor may actually guide them into the experience of examining each other's point of view and working through to some form of compromise or mutually agreeable solution. It may be necessary for him only to start the process during an interview and to let them continue it on their own. On the other hand, some couples will require the services of other professional persons. All couples should see a medical doctor for their premarital medical consultation. (See pp. 86-89.) A very few may need to see a psychologist for personality testing. For most couples the pastor will recommend certain basic reading, as suggested on pages 154-55. For others, additional books or selected chapters may be suggested in keeping with specific areas of need.

Make Plans

Finally the pastor aids the couple in utilizing the appropriate methods and resources and in making plans for their life together. This is a positive effort to make sure that the insights, information values, and so forth, discovered in premarital counseling are actually used to benefit the marriage. It is an attempt to evoke the couple to use these new understandings in specific plans they are making, so that premarital counseling "does some good."

It is not enough for the pastor simply to suggest certain reading, as relevant as this may be. He will need to check with the couple to see how much they have assimilated. He may find it necessary to point out certain information or principles which he thinks have significance for them and to assist them in using these in specific planning.

127

A case in point is the budget. For most couples, reading a chapter on money management does not give sufficient help. The pastor may need to review with them the items and amounts proposed and to explore the reality of these proposals. Together they may need to evaluate the way they plan to operate their finanacial spending plan—who does what and who is responsible to whom, and for what. (See pp. 32-36 in the engaged couple's manual.)

In addition to referring a couple to a medical doctor, the pastor will want to check with each person to see what he has learned and how well he can utilize the information. Most likely the pastor will find it necessary to supplement the doctor's counseling. For example, he may need to give some help in certain areas such as attitudes toward sex or birth control.

Since most of what is recommended in the final four chapters on procedures and resources is primarily educative counseling, we now turn to problem-centered counseling in the next chapter.

Chapter 10
Problem-Centered Counseling

One of the functions of premarital counseling is to help persons solve problems in the area of preparation for marriage. When seen from this perspective, *premarital counseling may be described as a personal and dynamic process in which a pastor and one or more persons approach a mutually defined problem, with mutual consideration for each other, to the end that the person(s) is aided to a self-determined resolution of his problem, and that he become a more mature person, capable of sustaining more wholesome relationships, who in the future will be able to handle problems as they come along.* Let us examine briefly each part of this definition.

This chapter is not an attempt to give a detailed description of the counseling process. That has already been done in a number of good books.[1] Rather this chapter is an effort to summarize some of

[1] For an overview of pastoral counseling, see Clinebell's *Basic Types of Pastoral Counseling*. Two basic books in this area are Seward Hiltner, *Pastoral Counseling*, and Paul Johnson, *Psychology of Pastoral Care*. A con-

the essentials of counseling and relate them to premarital counseling as such. Problem-centered counseling usually calls for more time than the suggested pattern of four or five interviews.

Primarily, this discussion focuses on the *person-initiated, problem-centered* aspects of premarital counseling. But it also describes some elements of the total counseling relationship which serve as the framework for the entire premarital counseling process in both its problem-solving and educative aspects. More specifically, as has already been indicated, this kind of counseling may occur in the midst of instructional counseling whenever a problem arises that the person or couple wishes to pursue further. Or it may happen when a person takes the initiative in seeking out the pastor for counseling because he has become aware of a problem as the wedding date draws near.

This was the case with a young man who approached a pastor, other than his own, six months before his proposed wedding date. The young man held rather liberal theological views and was active in a liturgical church. For about a month he had been engaged to a girl from a sectarian church. They had become involved in a very upsetting argument when she insisted on their attending an all-night singing convention and he refused. This argument brought out their theological differences. The young man felt their entire relationship was threatened by their religious differences and wanted help. It is interesting that he chose a pastor whom he believed held liberal theological views. (See implications of this on p. 136.)

A Personal and Dynamic Process

Premarital counseling is "a personal and dynamic process." It is not mechanical. It involves the face-to-face encounter of persons not things, and it has all the qualities of a person-to-person relationship. Primarily this is a personal relationship and not a set of techniques, although special methods are employed to facilitate the process.

Premarital counseling is also personal in the sense that each case

---

cise, simply written foundational book on marriage counseling is Dean Johnson, *Marriage Counseling: Theory and Practice.* For others, see the Bibliography.

is unique. For each person and each couple is different from all others and must be counseled on an individual basis. The counseling is personal also in the sense that we are dealing with the intimate and private concerns of persons.

Premarital counseling is dynamic and not static. This means that it is a moving process and not a stationary situtation. It is a relationship in which the pastor attempts to deal with all the forces at work in the situation, but especially the feelings. Premarital counseling is dynamic because it stimulates growth and development. It has power to change lives and relationships.

This kind of counseling is a continuing development in which feelings are expressed, understood, reflected, and faced responsibly, and in which problems are solved, decisions made, and actions taken.

Persons Involved

"A pastor and one or more persons" are involved in premarital counseling. As already indicated, premarital counseling may involve the pastor and only one person, or a couple, or other persons. On rare occasions there may be the "other woman" or the "other man" who is not being married. More often the other persons will be members of one or both of the the immediate families. When couples are very young their parents may be involved. When the persons are in the later years of life, their grown children, who feel they have a stake in the marriage and may oppose it, may be the other persons involved.

On a few occasions one or more sessions of premarital counseling may become family counseling in which the pastor sees at one time not only the couple, but also both sets of parents.

For example, this was necessary in a situation where communication had almost completely broken down between a young couple and their parents. Both of the young people were twenty-years old. The young man had one more year in college and his fiancée had two. When they insisted on getting married within three months, both sets of parents said no and refused to talk about any plans for a June wedding. But the young people were determined to go ahead with their plans with or without parental consent.

131

It was the girl's mother who asked the pastor to see the couple. She hoped he could "talk them out of it." The pastor said he would be happy to see them if they wanted to come in. He warned her that he would not tell them what to do but assured her he would help them review their readiness for marriage. The young people were willing to come in, for they hoped the pastor could help them secure their parents' approval.

The pastor saw the young people in four interviews, first together, then separately, and finally together again. He discovered that they were determined to go ahead with the wedding and were making responsible plans to that end. If their parents would not continue to finance their education, they planned for the girl to drop out of college and take a secretarial job until her husband graduated the following year. When he was able to support them, she planned to finish her education. This meant waiting more than three years to have children, and she had already seen her doctor and made plans to start on the Pill in another month. The couple evidenced genuine concern for their parents' views and feelings but felt there was no real reason for their opposing the marriage.

Between sessions with the young people the pastor saw both sets of parents separately, then together. The families had been friends for a number of years, and the young people had been dating more than two years. Interviews with the parents revealed their anxiety about the young people being "too young" and their desire to see them through college before marriage. But the parents had no further objection to the marriage. They objected only to the timing of the wedding; they wanted the couple to wait two years. They also expressed some fear that the girl might become pregnant out of wedlock if marriage was delayed that long.

The pastor felt the best way to resolve the impasse was to get all six persons together. They agreed. When counseling was started there had been almost no communication between the young people and their parents. By the time they all came together, everyone was eager to talk. And each person was less insistent on his previous position and more ready to understand the others' point of view. In the hour-and-a-half session all the parents except the girl's father were convinced that the young people were making responsible plans and should be supported in them. The parents agreed to finance their education on the same basis as when they were single and to go ahead with plans for a June wedding.

Following this joint session, the pastor saw the girl's father alone for one more interview. He still felt that his "little girl" was too young to marry, but felt that he would have to go along with the others' decision, and he reluctantly agreed to give her in marriage. Some time later the pastor had three more sessions with the young people, seeing them separately and together, to further their marriage preparation.

A Mutually Defined Problem

In problem-centered counseling the pastor and the person(s) "approach a mutually-defined problem." It is essential that the problem be clearly defined. If a person with the help of the pastor is still unable to identify and describe his problem, he may not be a proper candidate for counseling. His difficulty may be in the unconscious and he may therefore need the services of a psychiatrist instead of a pastor. In such instances, of course, a referral should be considered. Whenever possible, however, the pastor should consult a psychiatrist who can guide him in further exploration with the person before actual referral is made. This is one of many reasons why every pastor should maintain a continuing consultative relationship with a psychiatrist if at all possible.

It is also essential that the pastor and the person agree on what the problem is. If they are unable to agree on the nature of the problem, they may be working on different levels or even different problems and actually miss each other in the process.

One pastor discovered that this was exactly what he had done. A woman came to see him as pastor of the church she had been attending for about a year in the large city where she worked. She was engaged to a man who was in military service and unavailable for counseling. They were to be married in her hometown by the local minister in two months. This woman came to the pastor wanting to know how she could get her fiancé to agree to a large church wedding, as he preferred a brief ceremony in the pastor's study.

As she talked, the pastor discovered that she was a rather domineering person. In his own mind he identified the problem as growing out of the woman's trying to control the couple's total relationship. So he did his best to get her to be more understanding of her fiancé and to give him more freedom to be himself. After three interviews she thanked the pastor for what he had done, but said there was just one question she wished he could help her with: "How can I get my financé to agree to a church wedding?"

In counseling it is necessary to begin with the present problem, mutually agreed upon, and to work on that until the couple together or the individual agrees to move to another problem. Otherwise, very little progress can be made.

Another essential condition to problem-centered counseling is mutual consideration for each other. Mutual consideration moves in both directions—the pastor's attitude toward the person, and the person's attitude toward the pastor. As already indicated the pastor is one who cares, respects, accepts, and affirms the person in counseling. (See pp. 114-16.)

This consideration is expressed by the pastor in his not being shocked or repelled by anything the person or couple reveal to him, not because he is unfeeling, but because his concern for each person is so strong and genuine that he feels with and for another regardless of what has gone before. The person is not judged or condemned, but accepted as he is. He is not manipulated or told what to do, but his freedom and sense of responsibility are respected. He is treated as an autonomous person.

Keeping Confidences

This consideration is also expressed in the pastor's keeping of confidences. The pastor keeps confidences because of his respect for the person and also because he knows it is absolutely essential if counseling is to reach any significant depth.

A farmer in his late twenties had been seeing his pastor, trying to decide whether or not to become engaged to the girl he had been going steady with for more than two years. He was an active member of the church and a close friend to the pastor and his wife. He had asked the pastor to tell his wife about the counseling sessions. The pastor told his friend that he made it a practice not to share such information with anyone, not even his wife.

On his way to the fourth interview the farmer took a basket of vegetables to the parsonage and said something to the pastor's wife about seeing the pastor for counseling. He discovered that she did not know anything about it, that the pastor actually had kept their counseling relationship confidential. It was no coincidence that in the fourth session the farmer began to talk about a serious sexual problem. The pastor believes that the man never would have brought it up if the pastor's wife had known about the counseling sessions.

Consideration for the Pastor

For any significant counseling to take place, it is also necessary for the person to show some consideration for the pastor. In some instances it may be necessary for the pastor to help persons understand what form this consideration ought to take. He must help them accept him as a pastoral counselor and not expect him to be a psychiatrist or anyone other than the minister he is. For example, if transference in the psychoanalytic sense [2] occurs and the person unconsciously relates to the pastor as if he were some significant person in his childhood, the pastor, unless he is trained in depth psychotherapy, must direct the relationship back to the conscious level. If he is unable to do this, he should consider a psychiatric referral for the person, or at least consult a psychiatrist himself.

Also the person seeking help must be willling to work within the limits of the counseling relationship. Generally this means that counseling must be confined to the sessions agreed upon. The person must not make unreasonable demands on the pastor through numerous telephone calls or during chance encounters at various church meetings. He must accept the pastor as a counselor who helps him make his own decisions, but who does not take over his responsibility for himself.

[2] See Dean Johnson, *Marriage Counseling: Theory and Practice*, pp. 40-44, 110-13.

The pastor must always be on guard against being manipulated or controlled by the person in counseling. Trying to get the pastor to take sides when there are conflicts is one of the most common forms of manipulation. Perhaps this was one reason the young man with liberal theological views, who was engaged to the gospel-singing girl from a conservative church, sought out a pastor with liberal views. Of course he may have chosen the particular pastor because he was known to be a good counselor. But the pastor himself reported that the young man made several attempts to secure agreement with his position and to get the girl to change her views. The pastor refused to let himself be used in this manner and forced the couple to make their own decisions. In the process, each of them made some concessions and together worked out a compromise both of them could live with. (See p. 130.)

Self-determined Resolution

One of the pastor's main purposes in problem-centered counseling is to function in such a manner that the person "is aided to a self-determined resolution of his problem." This is the heart of successful counseling, in that the pastor is a *helper* more than a leader, a *servant* instead of a master.

The pastoral counselor is one who assists a person or a couple in making decisions or plans. He may guide them through the five basic stages of the problem-solving process as outlined on pages 109-11, but the actual choice of action is left to them. At no stage in the process does he take over their responsibility. Instead, he becomes a *facilitator*, not one who hinders or obstructs progress in decision-making and planning but one who eases the pressures and makes the process less difficult.

The counselor is also an *enabler*. He provides the opportunity for something to happen, the atmosphere in which it is easier to share. He offers the means by which problem-solving may be facilitated. He gives the encouragement and support to strengthen a couple in their planning. He may make suggestions, but they are free to accept or reject them. He may point out certain facts or forces he thinks they are overlooking, but they must decide what to do about them. In short, they are helped to make a self-determined resolution of their problem.

Trying to Do Too Much

Many pastors, however, make the mistake of trying to do too much for couples they marry. Some of us are so afraid we may fail that we overdo it. We seem to be so obsessed with the necessity to succeed that we are afraid to let a couple make their own decisions. We are afraid to give them the freedom to fail. It may be that we can do our best work only when we can give couples the freedom to fail. Otherwise they are not free at all. Some of us act as if everything depends on us, as if we do not trust God to work in the lives of the two persons entirely apart from our efforts.

The resolution of a problem may be that the problem is actually solved. On the other hand, it may mean accepting the fact of a difference and deciding to be willing to live with it. Or, it may be acknowledging the fact that a condition will continue to exist and learning how to cope with it. Ideally, the resolution of problems in premarital counseling should be some form of mutually satisfying arrangement or agreement between the persons counseled.

Beyond Problem-Solving

Beyond problem-solving, as important as that is, a greater concern is that premarital counseling will help couples to become more mature persons in the process. The way the pastor conducts the counseling sessions—the way he helps a couple solve their problems—determines whether they become dependent on him or are strengthened to work out their life together. This is why so much has been said in the foregoing paragraphs about the pastor assisting persons and couples to arrive at a self-determined resolution of their problem.

To be sure, premarital counseling is not strictly insight counseling, for that takes as long time—more time than the limited number of sessions usually allows. But some clearer self-understanding should result for the persons being counseled. To be sure, emphasis is usually placed on problems in the couple's relationship rather than on personal internal problems; but, to some extent, persons may become more mature, more responsible in the process.

In spite of the limitations of premarital counseling which must be recognized, we believe that counseling can be conducted in such a manner that it will help individuals gain sufficient ego strength, self-understanding, and courage to risk an openness with each other that they have not known before. At least it can help persons move in this direction.

Premarital counseling can also contribute to a person's growing sensitivity to another's needs and can stimulate a willingness to respond with sympathetic understanding and love.

If all this can be done, we are not only solving problems, we are helping persons mature according to God's purposes for them.

Pastors are also concerned about helping persons to become capable of sustaining more wholesome relationships. Certainly we would not be interested in premarital counseling unless we believed that it could bring some improvement to the relationship of the couple, insofar as this is possible under the time limitations. In facing their differences and the accompanying tensions, the couple may begin to come to terms with their need for both intimacy and distance, and make a beginning at finding some mutually satisfying balance.

Even though the process will continue throughout the marriage, premarital counseling can sensitize two persons to the significance of each granting the other the freedom to be an individual while at the same time being related in such deep intimacy that each is truly known by the other. As a man and a woman work out their problems together, hopefully they will discover that their marriage is a relationship that cannot be taken for granted but is one that must be nourished and cultivated in order to grow and enrich their lives across the years. Premarital counseling cannot assure success, but it can help a couple to make a start in the right direction and to trust God for further guidance.

Finally, problem-centered counseling is a means of facilitating growth in persons so that in the future they will be able to handle problems as they come along. Couples are strengthened to stand on their own feet and to live their own lives instead of being made more dependent on their pastor.

Although the pastor should always be available when he is actually needed, the couple should not feel that they have to return to him every time a new problem arises. They should have developed enough inner strength as persons, grown enough in their relationship with each other, and learned enough of the skills of problem-solving that they are able to tackle their problems themselves.

Discourage Dependency

Some pastors, however, have such a strong desire to be needed that they encourage dependency. Such pastors feel "left out" when couples are able to work out their problems. Actually this skill in problem-solving should be a cause for rejoicing by both the couple and the pastor.

One pastor reported that a couple became so dependent on him that they returned for counseling almost every time even a minor problem came up. Before the end of their first year of marriage they had seen their pastor in four or five series of counseling sessions about finances, relatives, sex, work, and planning for children. He indicated that he did his best to get them to make their own decisions, but they kept coming back to him.

Shortly after their first anniversary the pastor moved to another church several hundred miles away. Both husband and wife were in tears in their anxiety over losing their counselor. They actually told him they were afraid they would not be able to work out their problems without his help. After he had been gone for about three months the pastor received a letter from the husband apologizing for having depended on him so much and saying that they were doing very well on their own now. "In fact," the man wrote, "I guess your leaving town was about the best thing that has happened to our marriage!"

CHAPTER 11
The First Interview

What is presented in these next four chapters is a model from which each pastor may develop his own plan of premarital counseling—one that seems most appropriate for him, taking into account his time and energy and skill as well as a couple's readiness and need. Some pastors feel that the plan given here is too idealistic. Others see it as a basic minimum program of premarital counseling.

For a variety of reasons there will be situations in which four or five interviews with every couple will not be possible. Adjustments in the basic pattern will be necessary. On the other hand, this basic pattern will not be enough for some pastors. They may already be giving more than four or five hours to each couple they marry. What is recommended here is a basic minimum which can be expanded as the needs of a particular couple dictate.

A minimum of five interviews is recommended as the usual procedure with most couples. In the first interview, the pastor sees the couple together. In the next two, each person is seen separately. They are together again for the fourth. The fifth interview is to be scheduled by the couple from one to six months after the wedding. Procedure for conducting each of these interviews will be described in some detail.

Encourage Early Contact

Couples should be encouraged to begin premarital counseling from six weeks to three months before the wedding. The best time is before the engagement, or as soon thereafter as possible, especially if the couple needs to face any serious limitations in their relationship.

Many of us learn about a couple's wedding plans only a few days before the event, and we are forced to do the best we can in the limited time available. How can couples be encouraged to make early contact with their pastor?

The pastor's wife may give invaluable help here. Often she is the first to learn that a wedding is coming up. One of the women in the church may share the news that "my daughter is engaged," or the young people may know her so well that they confide in her about their wedding plans. Or a telephone call may be received at the parsonage—a query as to the pastor's availability for a wedding at a specified time.

The pastor's wife may handle such contacts as daily routine, simply as a matter of scheduling an event on the church calendar. On the other hand, she may use them as a means of helping the couple anticipate premarital counseling. She can let it be known that the pastor would like to see the couple as soon as possible to help them prepare for marriage, and she can find out how he can contact them when he comes in. Whenever a call comes to the church it is important that the church secretary does the same thing.

The pastor can build a network of communication by alerting parents, teachers, and young adults of his interest in learning about an engagement. Some pastors put a note of congratulations and best wishes in the church newsletter or bulletin whenever they learn about an engagement—with the permission of the couple, of course. Most couples appreciate this kind of recognition by the church. If it is done for one couple, others begin to let the

141

minister know when they want their engagement announced.

Some pastors give books on wedding etiquette to the couple as soon as they hear they are engaged.[1] The word soon gets around among the young people of the church that the pastor has a good book on weddings that they should get before making their palsn. This encourages early contact with the pastor.

One of the most effective ways of encouraging early contact is open to the pastor himself.[2] Whenever possible he should be involved in special study courses for young people on preparation for marriage. In these courses it may be appropriate for him to explain what he does in premarital counseling and give some of the reasons why early contact is so important.

Sermons on marriage and family life provide another means for pointing out the importance of early contact with the pastor in preparing for marriage.

Early contact may also be encouraged through printed materials. A church library should contain some of the best books on preparation for marriage. These might carry an insert from the pastor indicating his desire to be of service to all young people planning to be married and his desire to see couples as early as possible. The distribution of pertinent leaflets for both young people and their parents may also encourage early counseling sessions.[3]

Many churches are now preparing and circulating policy statements regarding weddings. Certainly such statements should include the pastor's policy about premarital counseling. These might be printed in the church bulletin or newsletter several times a year to inform the general congregation.

Because so much happens during each interview, the pastor should keep a written record of each session. During the interview

---

[1] A good one for this purpose is Natalia Belting and James R. Hine, Your Wedding Workbook, 1963, or Elizabeth C. Pearce and Betty S. Rogers, Altar Bound, 1966. Order directly from the Interstate Printers and Publishers, 19 North Jackson Street, Danville, Illinois 61834.

[2] For suggestions see Family Ministry—Through the Church by Leon Smith and Edward D. Staples, Chapter X.

[3] For young people: "Twelve Reasons for a Conference with Your Minister Before You Marry," No. 3087-C and "If I Marry A Roman Catholic." For parents: "If Your Child Marries A Roman Catholic," No. 3103-C. All may be ordered from The Service Department, P. O. Box 871, Nashville, Tennessee 37202.

he may make a rather sketchy account by jotting down key words or topic sentences. After the session he can fill in with more complete statements.

It is unwise to try to keep in mind all that happens in each session. There is too much danger of forgetting some essential details or of confusing one person or couple with another. With certain couples these records may be of value not only in the immediate interviews, but also in any counseling sessions that may come months or even years later.

It goes without saying that any records must be kept confidential. No names or other identifying information should be included. Instead, code numbers should be used, just as on the Premarital Questionnaires in the engaged couple's manual. Instead of by names, a man may be identified as Mr. X and a woman as Miss Y.

They Come Together

In the first interview the pastor sees the couple together. Why is it best to see the couple together before seeing them separately?

The basic reason is to get them started together. This protects each person from any fear that the other has moved ahead of him. This precaution may be crucial if the man is from another town or another church or does not already have a good relationship with the pastor, as the woman is likely to have. It is important that they both feel they are making their preparations together. This makes it possible for them to decide together whether they will continue with the additional counseling sessions.

Coming together for counseling means two persons are identified as a couple. This minimizes any feelings of separation or isolation and may be especially significant if there is problem in any of the relationships involved. Being together may make it easier for them to focus on their relationship.

Together two persons support each other by their very presence. They feel more comfortable in the experience of seeing the pastor for the first time for counseling. They are usually uncertain enough about counseling and also anxious enough about getting

143

married without having to cope with the feeling of aloneness too.

Interviewing the couple together also gives the pastor an opportunity to observe their relationship to each other, rather than observing them as individuals. By seeing them together he may pick up clues about their compatibility or the way they treat each other.

Perhaps the main reason for seeing them together at first, however, is because of what happens to the couple as they share the experience. Each may stimulate the other to make a particular response. They may raise questions with each other that deepen the process of preparation. This kind of exchange is likely to stimulate deeper communication outside the counseling sessions.

What Should Happen?

At least six or seven things should happen in the first interview. Not all of these will be achieved completely, but the process should begin and be well under way before the end of the first session.

1. The pastor and the couple begin to establish a counseling relationship, with some measure of rapport achieved. (See pp. 113-20.) Without this rapport, nothing of any real significance is likely to happen in any of the sessions. The pastor provides a climate of trust in which open communication may take place. This climate depends, primarily, on the kind of person he is—caring, respecting, accepting, affirming—but also on the kind of response the couple makes to the pastor. To a lesser extent it depends on what the pastor does and how he does it—the way he listens, understands, and responds to the couple and to their feelings, the way he asks questions and responds to their answers.

2. The pastor structures the counseling sessions by letting the couple know what to expect both in the immediate interview and in the following sessions. Without some sense of organization supporting them, many persons are likely to feel at sea or have a sense of lostness in the new experience of a permissive counseling relationship. Along with all the flexibility and freedom they need to feel that what is happening is part of a plan and that there is

some sense of direction to it. They need to have some reassurance experientially that the pastor knows what he is doing and where they are going.

3. The pastor helps a couple review and begin to evaluate the preparation already made for marriage. (This and the following items are only listed here. They are discussed in more detail on pp. 126-28.)

4. He also assists in identifying and assessing the need for further preparation, both as individuals and as a couple, insofar as this is possible.

5. Based on this review and assessment, the pastor suggests appropriate resources or methods for meeting their needs.

6. More specifically, he helps the couple to understand the nature of marriage from the Christian perspective.

7. In most instances plans are made for the rehearsal and the wedding (and possibly for some adjustments in marriage).

It may seem that this is a great deal to do in one interview, and it is. This is one reason the first session should be scheduled for an hour and a half, whereas the other appointments are usually limited to one hour each. The first interview is only one step on a longer process, with at least three more sessions to follow.

Where to Start

The best way to develop a counseling relationship is to start at the point of the couple's interest.[4] If the chief concern is planning for the wedding, as is true for most couples, this is the place to begin. Be sure to take enough time to answer their questions without any appearance of rushing, but at the same time do this as briefly as possible. Time can be saved if the couple fills out the Wedding Information blank in the back of the couple's manual; however, because of the nature of some of the questions, this should be done at the end of the session. Or, the couple may take the blank with them, complete it, and return it to the pastor later.

[4] This is a description of the procedure for the usual first interview with a couple coming for counseling at the pastor's request. For a verbatim report of a first interview with an individual who took the initiative in seeking counseling, see Dean Johnson, *Marriage Counseling: Theory and Practice*, pp. 63-72.

Help Them Relax

If the pastor is a stranger to one or both persons, some time should be spent in getting acquainted. Help the couple to feel at ease and to relax as much as possible. To do this, ask some simple, easy-to-answer questions to find out what you can about them and their relationship, such as: How long have you known each other? How did you meet? When were you first sure that she (he) was the one for you? When did you get engaged? In this way, you begin to share in their relationship, something that means a great deal to them. You do this not out of curiosity, but out of a genuine interest in them and their love for each other.

Somewhere in this introductory period you may want to ask why they chose you as the pastor to perform their ceremony. This may be especially significant if they are not members of your congregation. Such a question may deepen your relationship. It may also give some clues as to problem areas to be checked out later. Caution is usually in order in this first interview. And probing for problems is out. Most likely, probing will threaten the relationship at this point. Problems will surface at the appropriate time, provided a sound relationship is established.

Review Preparation

In the first session you will also want to find out what preparation a couple has already made for marriage. This information can guide you in suggesting further steps to be taken. What courses in marriage and family life they had in high school or college? What reading have they done? How much, and at what level? (It is best to find out authors and titles, if possible.) How helpful do they feel their reading has been? Answers to questions such as these serve as guides to additional reading that might be recommended. (See pp. 154-55 for basic recommendations and the Bibliography for others.)

It is also well to know what counseling they have had with other professionals. A crucial question is: Have you seen your medical doctor yet? Since many couples will think of seeing their doctor only to meet the legal requirements for a blood test, the value of a premarital consultation may need to be stressed. (See pp. 86-89.)

It is well to be prepared to recommend a doctor who is known to be trained and competent to do this kind of work.

If time permits, the individual interview may be scheduled in two weeks. This allows time for the couple to see a doctor before the private appointments. It also leaves time for some of the reading. Scheduling the individual interviews after the visit to the doctor gives the pastor an opportunity to review what was done by the doctor and to supplement as needed. In addition, the pastor may be able to help the couple assimilate and utilize information given by the doctor.

It is also appropriate to check on some of the plans the couple are making for marriage, primarily to see where they are in their planning rather than to give much specific help at this time. If a great deal of help is needed, additional counseling sessions will have to be scheduled of course. Specific questions may be asked about such matters as plans for a place to live, work, finances, sharing household responsibilities, in-laws, friends, education, community activities, recreation, or religion.

Use Questionnaires

One of the best ways to discover how to be of further help to a couple is to use the Premarital Questionnaires in the back of the couple's manual To Love and to Cherish. Using the questionnaires will be helpful to both the pastor and the couple.

1. The questionnaires save time. In the twenty or thirty minutes it takes to fill out the forms, the couple gives the pastor information that could only be obtained in four or five hours in conversation. At this stage most couples are eager to save time; and the busy pastor needs to save time, too, without jeopardizing his usefulness to the couple.

2. The questionnaires give each person an opportunity to become involved, in a serious, systematic way, in marriage preparation—in reviewing their readiness for marriage and in indentifying areas of need or further preparation. In filling out the questionnaires most persons discover items which they had not thought important, and are motivated to work on them.

3. The questionnaires stimulate communication. Usually, just as soon as one person completes the form he is eager to know how

the other person responded to certain items. Then the questions fly, "I didn't know you felt that way. Why did you say that?" Real encounter may be under way—and most of it entirely outside the appointed sessions.

4. Use of the questionnaires also enables the pastor to sort out a few major areas of need on which he can concentrate attention in the remaining interviews. They give him an overview of some pertinent influences in each person's background and some insights into the way they are adjusting to each other—strengths and weaknesses of the persons and of their relationship.

If the couple's manual has not been given to the couple previously this should be done during the first interview. Some pastors prefer to remove the questionnaires from the manual before giving it to them. This makes it possible to separate the forms and give them to each partner individually.

It is best to ask the couple to fill in the forms while in the pastor's office, perhaps at the end of the first interview. This assures the pastor that each person answers the questions alone, and that the questionnaires are left with him. If necessary, however, they may be taken home to be completed. If so, they can be enclosed in envelopes addressed to the pastor to facilitate returning them directly to him as soon as possible, at least the day before the next interview.

In any case, the partners should be carefully instructed to complete the forms according to the directions at the top of the first page. It is absolutely essential that each person fill out the questionnaire without help from the other. Once they have completed the forms, however, they should feel free to discuss them all they like. In fact, they should be encouraged to do so.

Before giving out the questionnaires the pastor should fill in serial numbers for each person in the upper right-hand corner. Each serial number is identified by name and address in the pastor's confidential file. He may call attention to the fact that no names appear on the forms. This assures the couple that responses are confidential; they are for his use only. Of course he will discuss each person's questionnaire with him in the private interview. Without violating confidences he will also discuss issues raised by the other person's different answers.

Suggested Procedures

Here are two ways this may be done in the individual interviews. First, in the area of background, Question 5 may reveal a difference in religious outlook. The pastor may simply ask the person to tell him how he feels about religious backgrounds, and take it from there.

A second approach may be in the area of relationships. Question 27 is: Have you planned your budget? Say the man answered yes and the woman no. Without telling the woman how her partner responded, the pastor may say, "You indicated that you have not planned your budget. Can you tell me if you have talked about finances at all?"

She may reply, "Oh, yes, we've decided to have a budget, but we haven't decided on any amounts yet. We are not even sure what items should be included. Can you help us with that?"

The pastor may give a positive response and suggest that they can best do that in the next joint interview. He may call attention to the suggestions on page 34 in the couple's manual or give her a budget form from which they may work out specific amounts. In the discussion the pastor may discover that the man checked yes because they had decided to have a budget. Thus there may be no real conflict here. Yet further work is indicated for both the pastor and the couple.

Review Both Questionnaires

The pastor needs to have both questionnaires returned to him in time to go over them carefully in preparation for the individual interviews. With some experience and careful concentration, he can do this in fifteen to twenty minutes.

Privately the pastor checks one form against the other, item by item, for agreements and differences. Agreements may indicate strengths that can be developed, and the differences, problems that require further attention. It saves time to make notes of items to be discussed directly on the questionnaire as the comparison is being made. This is especially helpful when partners give different responses. It is best to use a different colored ink in making these notes.

Every question on the forms is important, but of course some

149

are more significant than others. The actual value of each one is closely related to the needs of the particular couple answering them. Generally the significance of each question is discussed in a number of college textbooks on education for marriage.[5] Every pastor should be familiar with several of these in order to be aware of the potential significance of each question.

Because of their interrelatedness some questions should be viewed in clusters, such as the marital status and condition of the parents' marriages (Questions 14 and 15), and those relating to the individual's childhood (11, 12, 13, and 16). Such questions, however, must also be related to other factors such as the person's education, especially if a functional course on preparing for marriage was included. Such a course might help to overcome some negative conditioning in childhood.

Other examples of clustering are found in those questions related to affection and sex (30 to 34) and disagreement (36 and 38). A particular question like number 26, on the wife's working, should be associated with others like number 35, planning for children, and number 34, on child-spacing.

Compare Responses

In comparing one person's responses with the other, the overlapping of questions such as number 28 on household responsibilities should be checked for differences and similarities in role expectation. Another example of related questions is number 29, on activities in which the couple participates, and number 38 on disagreements. A good way to make this comparison is to copy onto each form the response of the partner, using a special symbol (such as "P" for partner) or a different colored ink.

Special attention is called to Question 38 on areas of disagreement. A difference in the way each person checked a particular item may point to a lack of communication between them. Or it may indicate a difference in understanding the item, rather than a basic difference in views on this question. Many

[5] Some of the best are Robert O. Blood, Jr., *Marriage*; Henry A. Bowman, *Marriage for Moderns*; Judson T. and Mary G. Landis, *Building a Successful Marriage*; and Paul H. Landis, *Making the Most of Marriage*.

couples check for almost half the items in the first column, "the matter has not arisen," and almost half in the second column, "we agreed." For adequate marriage preparation every one of these items should be faced one way or another. Very few couples actually agree on all of these. But many persons come to marriage with only superficial consideration given to many of these items so that they are unaware of much difference. A little more depth exploration may show more disagreement.

In this connection the last two columns under Question 38 are very important. One person may feel that a particular item has been discussed only superficially, while the other rates it "discussed in depth." The person who rates a discussion as superficial may feel that a deeper exploration is needed. Each area of disagreement should be noted and worked through.

Actually, a couple indicating much disagreement in several areas may have learned how to handle their differences and thus are in a stronger position than some others who are not aware of their disagreement. Of crucial significance, of course, is the way disagreements are faced or settled (Question 36). The premarital counseling session may be the occasion for learning more constructive ways of handling differences.

The pastor does most of the work suggested above between the first interview, when the questionnaires are given out, and the second and third sessions, when they are discussed with each person in the individual interviews. Further reference to the use of the questionnaires will be made in the next chapter on the individual interviews.

There is more work to be done, however, in the initial interview. Some pastors check on the couple's role expectations. Most pastors review the couple's understanding of the nature of marriage and of the vows to be taken. The possible interviews in the remainder of the premarital counseling process should be outlined and scheduled. Certain reading may be suggested.

Role Expectations

Some pastors prefer to focus on husband and wife role expectations. A number of paper and pencil tests are available in this area. One that is recommended is "A Marriage Role Expectation

151

Inventory" by Marie S. Dunn.[6] This inventory contains two forms, one for the man and one for the woman, to be filled out individually. Each form contains seventy-one statements of various roles of husbands and wives. Each person indicates his level of agreement or disagreement with each statement. He can do this easily within an hour.

After the pastor scores the inventories he may discover that a particular couple needs only a little help. Others may need a great deal of guidance in facing differing expectations. They may need help in recognizing their conflicting role expectancies and the adjustments that may be necessary in their marriage.

Why a Religious Ceremony?

One way to get at a couple's understanding of marriage is to ask why they want a religious ceremony or a church wedding. Some will respond that they would not feel married otherwise. Some will be frank enough to admit that they do not care, but their parents insist on it. Some will not know any special reason; they just think that is the way to get married.

The pastor may need to sharpen the issue by asking why they did not go to a justice of the peace or other civil servant, instead of coming to him. This is one way to point up the difference between a civil service that would join them in a legal contract and which may be dissolved on certain grounds, and a religious ceremony in which they commit themselves to a covenant relationship. This may open the way for a full discussion of their understanding of the religious significance of marriage.

Use the Marriage Ritual

Another possible approach is to review the marriage ritual. Unless the words are reviewed carefully in the premarital counseling session, they may not be heard at the wedding. (See interpretation in the couple's manual, Chapter 1).

Two weeks after a pastor had married Mary and John, he performed another ceremony at which John was an usher. During

[6] Available with "Teacher's and Counselor's Guide" from Family Life Publications, Inc., Box 6725, College Station, Durham, North Carolina 27708.

the reception John quizzed the minister, "Did you use a service different from the one you used at our wedding?" The pastor assured him that he used the same ritual, word for word. John looked at him for a serious moment, then grinned. "No kidding!" he exclaimed. "Did I agree to all that?"

In the informality of the counseling session the pastor has an opportunity to discuss the meaning of the ritual and the spiritual significance of marriage.

He may begin by explaining to the couple that as they read over the service together they should not worry about such details as where to stand, or when to join hands or exchange rings. They should be assured that instructions for all this will be given at the rehearsal. Now is the time to concentrate on the words, on what it means to be married according to these vows.

As the pastor reads the service through, the couple should be encouraged to interrupt at any point to ask questions or to make comments. Very few do either, however.

After the pastor has read the ritual through slowly, he may ask if they have any questions. If not, he can point out several of the most important statements or explain some of the symbolism in the ritual and discuss it with the couple.

Certainly each pastor will do this in his own way. But several key concepts may be emphasized, such as those mentioned on pages 63-64 and elaborated upon in the chapter "Toward a Theology of Marriage." Among these are the following:

1. *Monogamy.* "Wilt thou love her (him), comfort her (him), honor and keep her (him), in sickness and in health; and forsaking all other keep thee only unto her (him) so long as ye both shall live?"

2. *Vocation.* "It is therefore not to be entered into unadvisedly, but reverently, discreetly, and in the fear of God."

3. *Covenant relationship.* "Having duly considered the holy covenant you are about to make, you do now declare before this company your pledge of faith, each to the other."

4. *Other elements* of Christian marriage. Personal commitment to God in Christ—"in the name of the Father, and of the Son, and of the Holy Spirit. . . ." Genuine love for one another—"to love and to cherish. . . ." A part of a Christian community—"be-

fore God and this company. . . ." With concern for others, in service to the community and world—"Thy kingdom come, thy will be done on earth as it is in heaven." The overall goal of their life together—"and live according to thy laws."

Schedule Interviews

Before the first interview ends the pastor should make a tentative assessment of the couple's readiness for marriage and their need for further preparation. Based on this, and within the limits of time available, he should decide how many interviews to recommend. He may suggest the regular series of one private appointment for each partner and a joint session before the wedding and one afterward.

If the need is indicated, he may recommend several additional appointments, either private or together. Or he may prefer to leave the exact number of appointments open until after the private sessions. In any case, he needs to schedule them with the couple and outline what may be done in these sessions. On the other hand, he may now, or later, decide to suggest one or more referrals for either or both persons.

Suggest Reading

Based on his assessment of the couple's need for further preparation, the pastor may recommend additional reading. This reading should be a part of the counseling process and not a substitute for it. Some reading may raise questions which should be discussed with the pastor.

When reading is used as a basis for discussion, couples are not as likely to put it off (and never get to it) as when left on their own. Also such discussion has the possible value of alerting the pastor to other areas of need for further help. Most pastors or church libraries have a number of good books which may be let out on a loan basis. If not, the investment in a few of the best books will provide the resources every pastor should use. Most pastors find that it is necessary to keep careful records of books on loan.

Before suggesting any additional reading, it is wise to find out just what reading a couple has already done. This may be only a few superficial magazine articles. On the other hand, some may have read the very book you offer, or even something better.

This is what happened to one pastor who gave an eighteen-year-old girl, just finishing high school, a fairly simple book of about 125 pages. When he asked how helpful the book had been, he was surprised to hear her say, "Not much." She had already read, rather carefully, the 700-page college text *Marriage for Moderns* by Henry A. Bowman!

Two basic books which may be used with most couples are *When You Marry* and *Being Married,* both by Evelyn M. Duvall and Reuben Hill. The first is for teen-agers who may be considering marriage; the second is for young adults.

An excellent and more recent book is *Your First Year of Marriage* by Tom McGinnis, although it was written primarily for those who have just married. Some may want to recommend one of the Duvall and Hill books several weeks before the wedding and follow it up with the McGinnis book afterward. It contains a strong emphasis on communication and problem-solving.

Most couples will need a book on sex. There are many good ones in this area. Many pastors find that Oliver M. Butterfield's *Sexual Harmony in Marriage* gives enough help without overdoing it. This is best for young people preparing for their first marriage. Couples entering their second marriage, however (or needing help sometime after marriage) may need more information from a book such as *A Doctor's Marital Guide for Patients* by Bernard R. Greenblatt.[7] Some pastors prefer this last book for use with all couples. Or the longer book *Sex in Marriage* by Dorothy Baruch and Hyman Miller, which gives more than three-fourths its 270 pages to other related areas of marriage and parenthood. A good plan is to suggest to a couple that they keep the book on sex and return it a month or so after the wedding. Usually other books are returned before the wedding.

---

[7] Available to professionals only from Budlong Press, 5428 North Virginia Avenue, Chicago, Illinois 60625. Also recommended is John E. Eichenlaub's *The Marriage Art.*

CHAPTER 12

The Private Interviews

The second and third interviews have much in common, and can be considered together here. These are the private appointments in which the pastor sees each person alone.

Since the woman is more likely to be a member of the local congregation, the pastor is probably already acquainted with her. But he may not know the man. If this is true, it is usually better to see the man first, unless there is some special reason for seeing the woman before him. As a general rule, it is best to see the one who is not as well known by the pastor. This gives the pastor an opportunity to further strengthen the relationship. If he is equally well acquainted with both persons, the order of the appointments is a matter of convenience.

Why Private Appointments?

In the private appointments the major concern is still the marriage but it is seen from the individual's point of view, and there are distinct advantages in seeing each person alone.

Strengthen the Relationship

We have already suggested that the private appointment is an opportunity for the pastor to strengthen the counseling relationship with each of the partners as individuals. Here, more than in the joint interview, the individual may come to feel that "the pastor does care about me as a person—my feelings, my needs, my aspirations—as well as about our marriage."

Some sense of relationship has already been established in the first joint interview. But the individual interview is making a new beginning on a one-to-one basis. This one-to-one relationship is very different from the pastor-couple relationship. It adds a new dimension to the total counseling relationship. Now the pastor can concentrate his full attention on one person, and a deeper and more inclusive relationship is possible. Now the person is free to concentrate on his own feelings about anything under consideration, and on helping the pastor understand what he means instead of wondering how his fiancée is interpreting everything that is said, as he may have done in the joint interview.

This session gives the pastor an opportunity to get to know the individual as a person. He may want to recheck impressions gained in the previous joint interview.

The Individual's Preparation

This is also the most appropriate time to focus on the individual's preparation for marriage. All of the functions of premarital counseling may be carried out in the private session but with special reference to the individual. This setting provides the opportunity for the individual with the help of the pastor to review his own readiness for marriage. Together they may identify and assess his needs for personal growth or treatment or further preparation for marriage.

The pastor may also recommend certain resources on marriage preparation for the individual or help him to assimilate and use such resources.

Stimulates Communication

The private appointment stimulates communication. The one-to-one relationship makes it easier for a person to bring up certain problems or issues that he would find difficult to mention in the presence of his fiancée. Discussing these with the pastor may strengthen him to talk them through with his fiancée later.

The individual may need the pastor's help in learning how to deepen communication and actually come to grips with the causes of a problem. A couple may have become so irritated by a particular unresolved issue that communication has broken down, at least in this one area. By discussing the issue in the private session, the pastor may be able to break the logjam.

In the private appointment the pastor can raise the kinds of questions that are less likely to come up in the joint interview. This can have the effect of stimulating further thought and discussion on the part of the couple themselves.

Special Concerns

Certain subjects may be especially appropriate for consideration in the individual interviews. To be sure, most of these need to be faced by the couple together. But it may be wiser to initiate discussion in the individual sessions. Among these are such subjects as helping the individual understand what he brings to marriage as a person, and some aspects of adjustment which a couple may be too sensitive to talk about, such as personality characteristics, sex, in-laws.

For example, a person who feels some resistance to his future in-laws might hesitate to bring this up in the joint interviews but would feel fairly free to discuss it with the the pastor alone. Or, he may be slow to get into any discussion that might imply he is inadequate for marriage, or which might be interpreted by the other person as a reflection on him as a person.

Open-ended

Still another reason for the private appointment is that it facilitates the addition of interviews if some problem arises that calls for extended counseling. The pastor can simply suggest one or more additional appointments. This is more likely to be accepted by the person as a logical extension of the present pattern.

If, on the other hand, the usual pattern is for the pastor to see the couple together every time, it may be awkward to suggest a private session for one person. The person is likely to think there must be something terribly wrong with him that he has been singled out for a special session.

Suggested Procedure

How does one go about realizing some of the possibilities in the individual interview?

Since the pastor is aware of the fact that the individual appointment adds a new dimension to the counseling relationship, he will do all he can at the beginning of the session to put the person at ease. In a warm and friendly manner he will let the person know that he is glad to see him and that he appreciates the privilege of sharing in this preparation for marriage.

Reflect Feelings

Helping a person to be comfortable in the counseling session means being sensitive to his feelings, even if they are negative feelings of resistance to the counseling or to the pastor. Reflecting these feelings verbally brings them out into the open where they can be faced and talked through. Frequently negative feelings subside when they are reflected, not because they are surfaced and then brushed aside, but because the experience of hearing his feelings responded to in this manner gives a person a sense of being understood and accepted as a person. The resistance may have arisen originally because he expected the pastor not to understand him, or to reject him.

Structure the Session

Sometimes a person feels uncomfortable in counseling because he is not certain what is about to happen to him. This fear of the unknown can be allayed by giving some structure to the session. The pastor can indicate some of the purposes of the conferences and point out some of the things that may be done. These might include reviewing the questionnaire, checking on the visit with the doctor, discussing the reading suggested earlier, or talking about specific subjects.

Within this framework the pastor can let the person decide where they might begin. This opens the way for the individual to

159

bring up any problem or issue that he wants to talk about. If nothing comes as a result of suggestion, the pastor might proceed with the questionnaire.

Premarital Questionnaires

In reviewing the Premarital Questionnaire it is best to begin with the earlier questions about the individual's background. This helps the pastor to understand the person at the same time that he is helping the individual understand what he brings to marriage. This review should also include a comparison of the significant factors concerning similar items on the partner's questionnaire, again without the violation of confidence.

Before the session begins the pastor prepares for it by noting items that seem to call for further discussion. For a particular individual most of the items will not be important enough to mention. But seemingly inconsequential items can take on crucial significance because of the other person's responses.

For example, there may be nothing unusual about the fact that a woman is twenty-two years old. But, if her partner is thirty-five, this calls for some consideration. If either person has been divorced, this should be checked out according to "church standards" as well as the personal needs of the couple. If one of the persons has been recently widowed, it may take more time to work through his grief problem than to deal with a divorce.

What is suggested here is that it is not enough to take the simple facts on the questionnaire at face value. It is the *meaning* of these facts to one or both persons that is important. For example, what is the meaning of the couple's religious and educational backgrounds? In many instances it may be enough for the pastor to call attention to a certain response and ask what effect the person thinks this may have on their marriage.

The Individual's Background

Because of the possibility that some background influences might cause tension in marriage, some questions may need rather extended discussion. This would be true if a man with certain fixed ideas of husband-wife roles is marrying a woman who plans to work outside the home, as many wives do today (Question 26).

The man may be conditioned against housework (Question 7), which he might have to share if his wife works (compare Question 28), or against women working generally (Question 8), which he might have to learn to accept. This kind of situation should be faced and worked through in premarital counseling, perhaps first with the man alone and later with the woman, or with both of them together. If responses to Question 9 on the questionnaires indicate a wide divergence in economic backgrounds, this may indicate the need for adjustment.

Further exploration is called for when Question 12 reveals an unhappy childhood. Or when the questions about one's parents (Questions 14 to 16) report any negative conditioning. This may be true also when Question 13 indicates "very few" friends, especially if one's partner reports "many."

Relationship Questions

The private appointment may be the best setting for checking on relationship questions such as number 24, on how well the partners get along with their prospective in laws, and number 23, on the parents' feelings about the marriage. Special problems may be expected if there is parental disapproval. These may take on special significance if the persons rated any one of them differently.

In this connection also compare Question 24 on one form with Question 16 on the partner's form. This kind of comparison should be made, too, with Question 29 on both forms. The important thing is not the activities in which the partners participate, but how they feel about the participation.

Special attention should be given to the questions on affection and sex, numbers 30 through 35. The other person's response should be compared for possible differences in number 30, on affection. These responses may indicate that discussion is needed.

The pastor may want to evaluate responses to number 31 on courses or reading for understanding sexual relations as a guide in recommending further reading. Questions 32 and 33 about parents' discussion and feelings about sex should be checked for possible negative influences. These along with Questions 34 and 35

161

are most important in alerting the pastor to the need for help with sex information and attitudes.

Some young people still come to marriage with very little preparation in the area of sexual relations and without having had much help from their parents, who feel that sex should only be "tolerated." And yet our culture glorifies sex. No wonder many of our young people anticipate sexual relations in marriage with "mixed feelings" and are doubtful that their present knowledge of sex is adequate for marriage. Some persons, however, consider their knowledge of sex adequate for marriage (Question 34) and then request additional help by checking several items in the last part of this question.

Most Pastors Discuss Sex

It is heartening to note that more than 75 percent of former Methodist ministers discuss sexual relationships with the couples they marry. We should be prepared to provide information on all of the subjects listed under number 34. If we do not feel capable of discussing any one of these items, however, we may refer the person to a good book on the subject. Or we may be able to refer him to a competent medical doctor or to a clinic on family planning. (See earlier discussion on pp. 81-84.)

Counseling with Those Previously Married

Some pastors make the mistake of thinking that a person who has been married before does not need premarital counseling, especially in the area of sex adjustment. Experience indicates, however, that persons in the middle years need premarital counseling just as much as young adults—some, more. But counseling regarding sex, as any other concern, should be determined by the need of the particular person or couple. (See James A. Peterson, *Married Love in the Middle Years.*)

A widower in his middle forties, who had been married for more than twenty years, came for premarital counseling in preparation for his second marriage. In filling out the Premarital Questionnaire he reported that he thought his knowledge of sex was adequate for marriage. But on Question 34 he checked the item on "Sex reactions of the opposite sex." In discussing this with him his pastor mentioned the importance of the clitoris. "Clitoris?" he inquired, "what's that?" When the pastor explained, he was thoughtful for a moment. Then he said, half-talking to himself, "Well, I wonder if that's why my first wife didn't like sex." He turned to the pastor wistfully, "I wish I had known that twenty-five years ago."

As indicated above, we can anticipate that three out of four persons approaching marriage today will need some help in preparing for sexual relations. Generally speaking, if a person needs more help in this area than can be given in thirty minutes, it is necessary to add one or more additional counseling sessions. For if more time is taken to discuss sex in the regular four- or five-hour session, other equally important areas may be neglected.

Sex Knowledge Inventory

The Sex Knowledge Inventory,[1] called SKI for short, is a good resource for the pastor. It has two parts. Form X is a set of eighty multiple-choice questions on sex, mostly on sexual relations. Form Y is a test on sexual vocabulary and anatomy. It contains drawings of male and female anatomy, with parts to be identified and functions described.

A few pastors use the SKI with almost all the couples they marry. But it is recommended for routine use only if a minimum of six or seven hours is allotted to premarital counseling. The reason for this is, it takes considerable time to administer and interpret it.

To be administered properly the SKI should be taken *in the pastor's office* as a part of the premarital counseling sessions. Unlike the Premarital Questionnaire, it, because of its contents, should not be sent home. Most people can fill out Form X in about an hour; but women usually take a little longer than men to complete it. The pastor can score it in ten to fifteen minutes. But it usually takes at least an hour to go over it with each person. More time is required if there is very much discussion.

[1] Available with Marriage Counselor's Manual and Teacher's Handbook by Gelolo McHugh, 1968, from Family Life Publications, Inc., P. O. Box 6725, College Station, Durham, North Carolina 27708. A much briefer Sex Knowledge Test is available from Sexology Corporation, 200 Park Avenue South, New York, New York.

Since the decision to use the SKI may not be made until the private appointments, it may be difficult to schedule it. In most instances, however, the man and the woman may come to the office together for their individual interviews. While one is seeing the pastor, the other may be taking the SKI. Similar to the procedure for using the Premarital Questionnaire, the pastor should have time to review both inventories before discussing it with either person. Again, this material will be confidential. But the pastor should know the needs of each person before trying to guide one of them in being understanding and helpful to his partner.

Some Need More Help

As she approached her second marriage a woman in her late twenties needed a great deal of help in the area of sex. Before her divorce two years before, she had been married for six years, and had one child. One of the main reasons she had divorced her husband was sexual abuse. This was confirmed by her physician. She said she had not experienced an orgasm since the child was born, less than two years after their marriage, and no more than three or four times during those first two years. Even though she said she knew that sex was supposed to be a satisfying experience for women as well as men, the way she had been treated by her husband had so conditioned her against sex that she wondered if she could ever enjoy it, even with her new husband, who was a very gentle and considerate person.

Fortunately, the couple came for premarital counseling three months before the wedding, largely because the woman knew she had a sex problem and had discussed it with her partner. In addition to the two joint interviews and the two individual sessions, her premarital counseling included the SKI and six additional sessions, primarily on sexual attitudes and practices.

Even though the man indicated no special needs in the sex area, he also took the SKI and had three additional individual appointments. He did this in order to be able to understand what his future wife was experiencing and to learn how to be more helpful to her. Happily, within two months after marriage they reported some progress toward a mutually satisfying experience.

How do we decide whether to give the SKI? Of course the pastor will have to sense the need of each person as they discuss sex. But he can get some guidance from the way the person answers the sex-related questions on the Premarital Questionnaire. Generally, if any three of the questions get negative responses, this alerts the pastor to discuss with the person the possibility of taking the SKI.

Several examples may clarify what is meant. If a person has done little or no reading, has had little or no help from parents, and has a mother or father whose attitude toward sex is only "tolerating" or "rejecting," then that person may need the SKI. The same is true of a person who does not know how his parents feel about sex, and who has "mixed feelings" himself. Also, anyone who asks for additional help in as many as three areas on Question 34 may indicate that the SKI should be suggested; and certainly one who anticipates sexual relations either with "mixed feelings" or "somewhat fearfully," or who considers his present knowledge of sex inadequate, or is doubtful about it should be appraised of the SKI possibility. A majority of men request "help for partner" on Question 34, but of course this should be checked out with the woman herself. Some may need information but will not accept it. We want to offer as much help as is acceptable, but no more.

Review Visit to Physician

As a part of the discussion of sex the pastor can inquire about the visit to the medical doctor. This may be done in such a way as to make it easy for the person to bring up any questions in this area that he did not complete with the doctor. A well-qualified physician may have completed a full health examination for both persons, as well as a vaginal examination for the woman, and given the couple a good report. He may have prescribed a contraceptive, perhaps the Pill. But he may not have had time to discuss such matters as facilitating first intercourse, the importance of foreplay, the timing of intromission, position, or frequency. The pastor may need to do some of this. Or he may indicate where supplemental help is available in reading resources. He may also be able to help a couple to internalize information given by the physician.

We must recognize that most physicians—even those qualified

165

to do the premarital consultation—are so busy these days that they do not always take time to answer a couple's questions sufficiently. Or, knowing how busy the doctor is, a couple may hesitate to take his time. Frequently they have some questions about sex for their pastor which they did not ask their doctor. These questions may be in the area of attitudes and morals. Some couples, for example, still wonder what the church's policy is on birth control. Or they may ask for further information or guidance in the sexual adjustment as indicated above.

Inquire About Reading

The pastor may also inquire about any reading that was suggested in the first interview. This may serve several purposes. One is to help the individual actually assimilate and utilize the information. Another is to remind him of the value of the reading and to encourage him to do it. Of course, this inquiry about reading should include any area of background or relationship the individual is interested in and not be confined to sex. Occasionally couples will request additional recommendations of reading material.

Imagine Disagreement

But what if the review of the above items, including the Premarital Questionnaire, does not produce any significant discussion? One possibility is to adjourn the session before the hour is up. However, if this is done, something significant might be overlooked.

A case in point is the rather mature couple in their middle twenties, who showed no disagreement in any area on their Premarital Questionnaires. The pastor thought them a rare couple indeed!

In his private appointment with the man he said, "You indicate that you have had no disagreements, and that you do not expect to have any serious ones after you are married. What I want to ask you is this: *If you could imagine yourselves having even a minor disagreement over something, what do you think it might be about?"*

The young man thought a moment, mustered his courage, and replied, "She might be too bossy." The pastor invited him to explain what he meant. Gradually he opened up and reviewed some of the facts about his fiancée's family. Her father had died four years ago, but his insurance and her part-time work made it possible for her to finish college. Her mother had been an invalid for several years. He was proud of the fact that she had actually supported the family since she graduated three years before. And when married, they would continue to contribute to the support of her mother and her younger brother.

It was more difficult for him to explain that his fiancée had a little brother twelve years old. Because of the family situation she had been like a father and mother to the boy. Then the man came to the point as he said with deep feeling, "I guess I'm afraid she might treat me like a little brother." He sighed as though he was glad he had finally said it, "Yes, I'm afraid she might be too bossy."

The pastor explored these feelings with him. After extended conversation he finally reported, as if a light had come on, "You know, Pastor, I guess one of the main reasons I'm marrying her is that she's such a good manager." Then he added with a sly smile, "But she'd better not treat me like a little brother!"

In their fifth interview, almost six months after the wedding, this young man was almost exuberant as he remembered how the earlier premarital discussion had given him enough courage to talk with his wife about his fear of her bossiness and his appreciation of her managerial abilities. He felt that being able to talk about it together kept it from becoming a problem between them. If they had not brought it up, he felt he would always have been sensitive to any hint of control from her and would have found some way to strike back.

The pastor later reported that he believed this was one concern that never would have been brought up in a counseling session with both persons present. He believed it took the safety and the comfort of the private session to free the young man to discuss his problem.

Additional Sessions?

Sometime before the end of the private appointment the pastor needs to decide whether to recommend one or more additional

167

counseling sessions. Of course he will evaluate this recommendation with the person. It may be rejected, but the pastor is responsible for taking the initiative in suggesting further counseling. Whenever the need becomes evident and time is available, the appointments should be scheduled as soon as possible, for additional counseling may reveal the need for other help.

Similarly, in the private appointment the pastor may discover that one or both of the partners needs to be referred to another professional person or agency. In such a case, he should follow the best referral procedures. (See pp. 89-91.)

CHAPTER 13
The Fourth Interview

In the fourth interview the couple are together again. For most couples this session comes only one or two weeks before the wedding, so it is an opportunity for a last-minute check-up. Also, for most of them, this will be only one session. But for others, if they begin early enough to allow time for it, and if the pastor has time available, this "fourth interview" might be extended into several sessions, depending, of course, on the needs and wishes of the couple.

Again the word is flexibility of structure, to meet the needs of persons and not simply to fill out a prescribed pattern of sessions. If this joint interview should develop into several sessions and take place in several steps, what is described here should take place in the last stages of these sessions. At this time the emphasis is not so much on needs and problems—although there may be some—but on positive plans for the couple's future together.

Purposes

Basically, three purposes are to be achieved in this fourth interview. In addition, some of the tasks of the earlier interviews not yet

169

completed may be carried over into this session. But mainly this is a time to look to the future and to bring the premarital counseling sessions to a close.

1. This is an opportunity to bring the two persons together again to make plans as a couple for their forthcoming marriage.

The private appointments, just concluded, focused on the individual's feelings about himself as a marriage partner, about his future partner, and on his own views of marriage. For many, these interviews may have majored in problems and tensions, with only minor attention given to their strong points and to planning together. This session is the time to stress their strengths and to enhance their potentialities for growth together. This is the time for a positive emphasis on their future together.

2. Insofar as possible, this is also the time to help a couple complete the tasks of premarital counseling together. This purpose may be accomplished, more specifically, in five ways:

a. The two persons continue to review critically their readiness for marriage, but hopefully the emphasis is now on their readiness to move ahead together. In a very few instances there will be exceptions, for some couples may find that this session is the time for a decision not to get married or to postpone marriage. If not done before, the pastor now finalizes his own decision as to whether to marry the couple or not.

b. This is the time to summarize their learnings from earlier experiences of identifying and assessing their needs, stressing now their strengths and the inner resources they have developed.

c. As they face the future, the pastor helps them discover resources available in the church and community which may enrich their marriage, both by what they receive and by what they give in serving others.

d. The pastor continues to help them make plans for their life together. He may do this by reviewing some or all of the developmental tasks, or by concentrating on a few specific

170

areas of adjustment such as money, planning for children, religion.

e. The pastor helps the couple continue their efforts to solve problems. These may be problems that have not been faced previously or which are yet to be worked out. But, with a look to the future, he also helps the couple to be realistic in expecting to continue to have problems after they are married and points out resources for handling such problems. He does this so that they will not feel their marriage has failed the first time they have an argument.

3. A final purpose of this fourth session is to make a tentative closing of the premarital counseling. The word tentative is used deliberately. Only the pre-marriage phase of premarital counseling ends with this session. The pattern here recommended includes a fifth interview to be scheduled from one to six months after the wedding. This plan is a definite effort to keep the counseling relationship open so that the couple will find it easy to return for continued counseling whenever they wish. Therefore some specific reference should be made to the fifth interview and directions should be given as to how they can make the contact.

Counseling After the Wedding

In some special situations most of the "premarital" counseling may be done after the wedding. Some couples may notify the pastor of their wedding plans too late to allow for more than one joint session beforehand. After the wedding, it may be appropriate to have one or more of both the individual and the joint sessions. These may be patterned very similarly to the premarital sessions. But, of course, they will deal with the here and now of their relationships.

Some pastors feel this kind of preventive counseling is actually superior to the pre-marriage sessions because the pastor can deal with the couple's present relationships. Too much should not be expected, however, in situations where couples are simply not interested in counseling. This may be the reason why many do not notify the pastor of their wedding plans early enough to permit premarital counseling. Very few of these disinterested persons follow through with counseling even after the sessions have been set up.

Continuing Concern

Technically, premarital counseling in pre-marriage sessions closes with the fourth interview. But, as noted above, the overarching pastoral-care relationship continues. It is appropriate, therefore, that the pastor let the couple know of his continuing interest in them and their marriage. Some reference may be made to his looking forward to seeing them in the congregation and at other appropriate church or community meetings in which they may be involved.

As a part of his concern for the couple the pastor should see that they are helped to join special couples' groups or classes in the church. Many of them—especially younger couples—are hesitant and may find it difficult to make the transition from a single to a married group. Needless to say, this is an opportunity for ministry on the part of couples already in such groups to reach out to the newlyweds.

Some pastors make it a practice to remember all couples on their wedding anniversaries in some special way. This may be done by sending them a greeting card or by writing a personal letter. This is one way to keep the possibility of counseling open, not by extending a direct invitation to them to come in but by communicating a continuing concern for their marriage. This practice may have real value for members of the pastor's congregation, but questionable value for couples who are members elsewhere.

Perhaps a word of caution should be entered here to discourage any efforts to make couples dependent on their pastor. Appropriate forms of ministry are recommended that will help couples in continuing to mature.

Procedures

There are several ways the purposes of this interview may be achieved. First, it may be best to review certain questions from the Premarital Questionnaire and any concerns that have come up in the individual interviews that need the attention of both persons. Also, the couple may need to face some specific questions together,

172

which may not have come up before, such as questions about budget, planning for children, or religious life. Third, they may summarize some of their learnings from the counseling sessions, which, hopefully, will furnish encouraging guidelines for the future. Finally, outstanding housekeeping details should be checked.

Review Questions

Reviewing the Premarital Questionnaires and details from the individual interviews will vary, of course, with each couple. But certain questions may be anticipated by the pastor and planned for after careful study of the forms. These should include any questions on which the pastor believes additional work is indicated.

Some of this additional work might be done during the premarital sessions when the pastor can help the couple work through the issues. Much of the work, however, the couple will have to do after marriage; in which case the pastor may call attention to areas of need for further growth. He may also make helpful suggestions as to how that growth and development may be facilitated. Often it helps for the pastor simply to alert couples to the fact that tensions may be expected in certain areas. Being so alerted is a kind of preparation for the experience itself. They are not taken by surprise, but are better able to proceed cooperatively with constructive action.

Background

Additional work may be needed also when there are marked differences in background. The questionnaire contains several possibilities of this type. Age may be an area of concern if the couple is very young, if they are old enough to be "set in their ways," or if there is a wide difference in age—especially if the woman is much older than the man.

Depending on the section of the country and the particular community the couple lives in, race or nationality may be an issue—especially if their backgrounds are different. A great deal of give and take may be required if there is much difference in their religious, educational, or economic backgrounds. This may be true also if one person is an only child and the other one comes from a large family.

Relationships

In the area of relationships there are many possibilities for further work. Four of these may be given special attention. The first is parental approval of the marriage. If this is a problem area, most likely it would have come out in one of the earlier sessions. But now it may need to be faced by both persons together. Even when there is no disapproval, many young couples may still need help in realizing that they are establishing a new family, and that their primary loyalty now is to each other and not to their parents. It is very difficult for some persons to make this adjustment.

The way a couple divides household responsibilities is another possible problem area. Each person's response on the questionnaire should be checked for agreement or disagreement on these role expectancies and their intentions to perform. Again, something may have been said about this in the private appointments. But unless both the man and the woman have worked these through on their own, now is the time to get further help from counseling together. Question 28 should also be related to Question 7 regarding the experience and feelings of each partner about housework.

Activities

Another important area of adjustment is highlighted in Question 29 regarding the partners' participation in certain activities, either together or separately. Perhaps more important is their feeling about the extent to which they share these activities. Certainly a couple must share enough common interests and activities from which to weave a relationship of durable quality.

Another crucial concern here is the extent to which one person grants the other the freedom to be himself. Some couples, therefore, will need guidance in cultivating common interests. Others may need help in learning how to release each other to develop personal interests. Ideally, marriage is a relationship which strengthens and sustains the individual in developing his most creative self.

Disagreements

Question 38 contains a number of possibilities for further work on disagreements. The pastor may review with the couple the various items both of them checked in the first column indicating no disagreement because the matter has "not arisen."

The purpose of this review is to see what progress they may have made between sessions in actually coming to grips with these disagreements. If they have not done their homework, the pastor may need to point out the significance of some of their disagreements and indicate ways they may expect to face them in their future relationship. It should be helpful also to compare those items checked "none; not arisen" and "none; we agreed" with the checks in the last two columns on the page. Many of the items may have been discussed only superficially and therefore may need further attention. This may be true also of some of the areas in which they indicate little, some, or much disagreement.

The most important thing in all of this is not simply to point out areas of disagreement. It is to assist the couple in finding ways of working out some of their disagreements and of coping with others.

The individual interviews may have revealed concerns that also need the attention of both persons in this fourth session. Perhaps in the private conferences the pastor sensed this need and suggested that the individual initiate discussion of the subject with his fiancée. Or the pastor may have encouraged him to bring it up in the joint interview if that seemed best.

If there is a crucial matter that needs attention and neither of the above courses of action has been taken, what is the pastor to do? To be sure, he must be careful to protect the confidential nature of the individual sessions. But without violating confidences he is free to bring up the subject in a general way and encourage the couple to talk about it together.

Face Specific Questions

A second way to try to achieve the purposes of the fourth interview is to help the couple face some specific questions together which may not have come up earlier.

Developmental Tasks

One procedure is to go over each of the developmental tasks to find out what plans the couple have already made and what additional help can be given in this session. Since the various tasks will be discussed briefly in the next chapter they are only listed here:

1. Developing and sustaining a Christian way of life
2. Providing the necessities of life
3. Earning and spending
4. Establishing husband and wife roles
5. Creating and maintaining communication
6. Meeting personal and affectional needs
7. Planning for children
8. Adjusting to relatives
9. Making and keeping friends
10. Taking part in community life

This approach has two advantages. It provides a comprehensive coverage of the most important tasks the couple will face in marriage. It also focuses on the future, on what the couple will be trying to achieve together after they are married. Since a developmental task is something the couple must do themselves, the pastor is limited in what he can do for them. But he can help them see the scope of their tasks in marriage, and he can give them some guidelines for approaching these tasks.

Three specific items, if they have not been worked through satisfactorily earlier, ought to be worked on in this session. They are finances, planning for children, and religion. (The comments given here supplement those made elsewhere in this manual.)

Finances

In discussing finances the pastor should be sure the couple consider earning as well as spending. This includes the wife's working and all this involves, as well as how her part of the income is to be used and how her working is related to planning for children.

This discussion should take into consideration the earlier comments about money, including the specific suggestions to be evaluated by the couple. In addition, the couple may want the pastor to review their budget.[1] In doing this he should be sure

---

[1] See Duvall and Hill, *Being Married*, pp. 227-70, or Duvall and Hill, *When You Marry*, pp. 175-97, also the manual for engaged couples.

they have not omitted some important items such as gifts, recreation, medical insurance, savings, and spending money.

Buying gifts for others can wreck a budget. The young couple are likely to have several friends getting married soon. And there is always the expense of birthdays and Christmas or other special occasions. Most couples make the mistake of thinking that they will not need very much money for recreation. They think they can save money on dating as soon as they get married. But they should budget for the kind of recreational and educational activities that they enjoy personally and that will strengthen their companionship.

A few couples may spend too much on insurance, but most will not be aware of the importance of medical insurance, especially if they have not had to carry their own before. Rates of group insurance available through the business where they work or through professional organizations should be investigated and compared with individual policies.

Of course it is possible to take all the joy out of living by overemphasizing savings. But most couples will need to be reminded of the importance of saving for emergencies and should be encouraged to put aside from 5 to 10 percent of their income as soon as they are able to do it. Another item often overlooked in budget making is allowances. Each person should have some spending money for which he does not have to account to the other.

The budget should serve two purposes. First, it is a guide to spending on which the couple have agreed in advance. Second, it provides a basis for reviewing spending at the end of the month and making whatever changes may be necessary.

Family Planning

Another specific item to be faced in the fourth interview by the couple together, if they have not done so before, is their planning for children. This subject is discussed briefly in the section on developmental tasks.[2] Although they may not have their first child

---

[2] See also Duvall and Hill, *Being Married*, pp. 375-91, and *When You Marry*, pp. 293-313.

for perhaps two years, there are four sound reasons for discussing this concern in premarital counseling.

The first is to help the couple arrive at basic agreement on how many children they want to have and when, even though they may change their minds later. The second is to see that they have adequate medical advice for their family planning. Third there may be several factors they should consider before making a decision to start their family, such as finances, wife working, further education, or living arrangement. And, fourth, to get the subject out into the open, they need to talk about these considerations, although the actual decision may be many months in the making.

Checking both partners' responses to the Premarital Questionnaire may reveal that they already agree on when they want children and how many children they want. If they did not agree, these questions may have already come up in the individual interviews. If not, the sooner agreement can be reached, the better. Question 35 should be checked with Question 26 regarding the wife's working and how long she plans to work.

Some women plan to work "indefinitely" but want to have children in two years. They may have forgotten to consider the temporary or long-term loss of income, and will need to be guided in doing some careful financial planning to cover this period. Some women plan to work only until the first child is born and do not expect to return to work until the children are in school. This has implications regarding their plans for the use of the wife's income during these early years; it should be used but preferably not for living expenses. If a high standard of living is established by living on two incomes, a necessary lowered standard of living in the future may be blamed on the child, especially if there is an unplanned pregnancy.

Adequate medical advice regarding birth control is important to every couple, but more so to couples in special circumstances. They need to feel secure about the method of birth control they use, so that they can be freed to enjoy sexual relations without any fear of conception. This is why the pastor needs to find out how they feel about the advice and prescription they have received from their doctor. This is especially true when couples have a special reason for waiting to have a child, such as waiting until the husband completes his education and they will no longer be dependent on the wife's income.

Some couples may still have questions about the morality of contraceptives and may want to know the church's stand on birth control. They may be encouraged by this statement from the Resolution on the Church and Family adopted at the 1968 General Conference:

Responsible Family Planning. In the Christian view, it is within marriage that children should be conceived, brought into the world as a precious gift in trust from God, and nurtured to full personhood. Responsible Christian couples may choose parenthood, determining the number and spacing of their children, or, for valid reasons, they may decide not to have children. Couples should use those methods of family planning that are medically and aesthetically best suited to their needs. Some couples who cannot have children of their own may decide on adoption, working through the most reliable placement agencies. We believe that responsible family planning, practiced in Christian conscience, fulfills the will of God. The present population problem calls for a continuing responsible attitude toward family planning.[3]

It is not too early for a couple to begin to think about some of the factors involved in a decision as to when to have their first child. Also discussion of timing in the premarital counseling session can lessen the possibility of accidental parenthood.

Parenthood should be seen as a Christian vocation. It should be entered into in response to God's call to join with him in the creative process, not only of bringing new life into the world, but also of helping that child to grow to full maturity as a person in Christ. This means checking out such factors as the physical and emotional health of both parents, but especially the mother, as well as educational and vocational plans, financial position, social conditions, and the needs of society, as well as personal preferences. A couple should be advised, however, not to wait too long to begin their family. If they wait for perfect conditions, they may never have any children. Most couples, however, need to

[3] *Book of Resolutions of The United Methodist Church 1968*, p. 91.

allow themselves at least one or two years to become adjusted to each other before taking on the responsibility of parenthood.

Religion

The area of religious life, as already suggested, includes more than devotional life and church relationships, important as these are. It is important for the pastor to help a couple realize that their marriage relationship may be a channel for God's love and that their marriage may be a means of service to the world.

The pastor may inquire about the devotional life of each person and his plans for spiritual growth after marriage. He may encourage couples to have daily devotions together. He may do this by letting them know that he will give them a book of devotions for the first four weeks of marriage, possibly *Whom God Hath Joined* by David R. Mace. It is best to give them this book with the marriage certificate immediately after the wedding, so they can take it with them on the wedding trip. This book has so much helpful material that some pastors give it to all couples they marry, not just to those who expect to use it as a book of devotions.

In reviewing church relationship the pastor needs to note how active each person is in his own church as well as to what church he belongs. If there are differences indicated, these may have been faced earlier. But this is the time for the couple to plan for their future church life together. The pastor may need to help them realize the significance of this aspect of their relationship, for many couples do not see the value of church participation.

God's Love and Purpose

This counseling session is also an opportunity for the pastor to help a couple rejoice in the fact that their relationship expresses God's love. God is love, and the source of their love for each other. God's love is unconditional—sacrificing, forgiving, sustaining, affirming.

Most important, however, is helping a couple realize that God has a purpose for their marriage—that their marriage is a means of service to others. The purposes of marriage include the ministry of husband and wife to each other and to their children. But it extends beyond this to fulfilling God's will for them in the world today.

One way to open up this subject is to review responses to some of the items in Question 38 of the Premarital Questionnaire—religion, values and life goals, political and social issues, and perhaps community activities. Another way to stimulate thought is to ask a couple what they hope to have accomplished in ten, twenty, or thirty years. What are they giving their life to? For most couples this may be an entirely new thought, and they may not know how to respond. But discussing their values and goals in life may help them begin to think about their marriage as a part of God's kingdom.

Summarize Learnings

In summarizing some of their learnings it is good to let a couple point out some of the main areas in which they recognize that additional work is to be done, and to go over some of the ways they expect to continue working on these after marriage.[4] Some of these may be differences or circumstances which they must accept as given and find ways of coping with them. Others may be disagreements or problems which they feel they can work out with more time and effort. Perhaps they have developed some skills in problem solving which should be undergirded. (See pp. 107-11.)

Not to be overlooked in this summary is a review of the strengths the couple have discovered or demonstrated. They should be encouraged to list these. The pastor can help them appreciate the value of these strengths in making their adjustments in marriage. He should also feel free to call their attention to any problems or strengths which they may have overlooked.

He may guide them in utilizing appropriate resources in the church and community. If the pastor "feels good" about the way these two persons have grown during the counseling sessions, he should say so. He should not hesitate to express positive evaluation whenever appropriate. A couple may have begun with several areas of tension or disagreement. In counseling they may have made considerable progress toward resolving some of these. Such positive

---

[4] See the chapters "Common Conflicts" in Duvall and Hill, *When You Marry*, pp. 199-217, and "Coping With Conflict," *Being Married*, pp. 273-94.

experiences should be noted and continued improvement encouraged.

This summary should include some mention of the crucial significance of communication in marriage, if sufficient attention has not been given to this subject before. If this is the case, more extended discussion is called for. At the least, the couple should be reminded of some of the important elements of communication.[5] Reference may be made also to some specific suggestions on how to face disagreements, such as the guides on "how to fight fair":

"Spell out exactly what you didn't like, and how you want things changed.

"Stick to the point and avoid side issues.

"Stay with it until you thrash things out.

"Go on to some simple next step for improvement.

"Get it out, don't let it fester.

"Attack the problem rather than each other.

"Avoid dragging in your relatives.

"Give each other cues as your tension lets up." [6]

To be sure, admonitions usually do not effect much change, but some couples may appreciate being reminded that a good marriage requires effort, they should be careful not to take each other for granted, and their marriage is worth working on together. They may also appreciate some guidance in how they can continue to grow in their relationship and find mutual fulfillment across the years.

Housekeeping Details

Some "housekeeping" details may need attention during this interview. These may be details regarding books, the marriage license, the rehearsal, the wedding, or pastoral services.

Books. Most pastors want each couple to keep the couple's manual *To Love and to Cherish*, and they may write a brief message of best wishes to them on the first page. Most books borrowed for

---

[5] See "Learning to Speak the Same Language," pp. 29-49, and "Reaching Decisions and Settling Disagreements," pp. 52-83, in McGinnis, *Your First Year of Marriage.*

[6] From *Being Married* by E. M. Duvall and R. Hill. Copyright © 1960, by D. C. Heath & Co., a Division of Raytheon Co., Boston, Massachusetts.

special reading should be returned whenever the couple finishes them or perhaps by the time of the rehearsal. (Some pastors prefer to make gifts of one or more books.) It is usually best for the couple to keep the books on sex and devotions until a month or so after the wedding.

If *Your First Year of Marriage* by Tom McGinnis is used, the couple may be encouraged to keep it longer or until the fifth interview. Or perhaps a better plan is to lend this book to the couple at the time of the fifth interview. Sometimes a couple finds one or more of these books so helpful that they want to keep them for further reference or to share with their friends. If so, the pastor can suggest that they purchase the books. Each pastor needs to keep records on his books, or he may lose many of them. He usually finds it necessary to follow up on at least half of them.

Marriage License

A good practice is to have the couple bring the marriage license to the pastor before the wedding, at least not later than the rehearsal. This could save an embarrassing delay of the wedding, since he is required to have the license in hand before he can perform the ceremony.

Rehearsal

The pastor can help the couple anticipate the rehearsal as preparation for the worship service that the wedding will be, and he can conduct the rehearsal accordingly. If the bride plans to have someone stand in for her at the rehearsal, as many do, at some time the pastor can help her walk through the service of holding hands and exchanging rings as the couple will do.

Wedding

Because of the excitement and strain the couple will experience during the wedding, the pastor should do all he can to reassure them explaining that he will guide them through each step of the ceremony and they need not worry about details. This kind of reassurance and attention to detail at this time can be very stabilizing and can help a couple to be more aware of the meaning of the vows during the service itself.

Pastoral Services

Before closing this interview, the pastor may check on some pastoral services that he might render the couple. For example, if they are moving to another community, he may be able to help them establish a relationship to a new church or to groups or persons in the new community. If they are going to college, he will want to find out how to keep in touch with them as well as how to help them become related to the religious group for married students on the campus.

Plan for Fifth Interview

Further plans should be made for the fifth interview to take place from one to six months after the wedding. The pastor must make it clear that he is leaving the responsibility for initiating the contact with the couple. He should help them feel free to call him at any time they wish. This fifth interview should be offered and anticipated, but the couple should not be coerced into accepting it.

The pastor should explain the nature of such an appointment. Most likely it will be a review of progress they are making in their adjustments with each other, very much as the pre-marriage sessions have been. Or, if appropriate, they may choose to use the time to work on one or more problem areas. If they want help with a particular problem, they should be encouraged to call their pastor immediately. It is very important, as mentioned previously, that this be done in such a manner that dependence on the pastor is not encouraged.

Prayer

Prayer may have been used in previous sessions whenever appropriate, but the pastor will probably want to close this final counseling session with a prayer of blessing on the couple and on their love and life together. He may actually pray the prayer for the couple in the ritual, instead of reading it. This may be the only time they will actually hear it, for they may be too excited at the wedding.

Generally, however, it is best not to begin an appointment with prayer. This focuses attention on God, and we are not sure what the person's attitude toward God is. He may see God as a stern judge, who is condemning him for something he has done. This image makes him hesitate to bring up certain negative acts or feelings that may need to be discussed. It is better to let God's love be felt in the presence of the pastor himself.

When prayer is used at the end of a counseling session, the pastor should try to reflect whatever struggles or achievements have been discussed, or whatever resolutions have been made. Obviously, prayer should not be used as a means of talking a person into something, or for trying to use God to get a person to come around to the pastor's point of view, however subtly this may be done.

Chapter 14
The Fifth Interview

The fifth interview takes place from one to six months after the wedding. Actually this is an optional interview, and some couples will choose not to come for it. Nevertheless, the possibilities it offers for real help indicate that it should be anticipated as a probability for all couples.

Major Purpose

The major purpose of this fifth session is to keep the counseling relationship open, and to make it easy for the couple to return to counseling if they need and want it. If a problem comes up that calls for counseling, the couple does not have to hesitate to contact their pastor. They already know that the interview is open for them.

For example, when a problem arises one person may say to the other, "The pastor is expecting us. Don't you think it's about time we called him for that appointment?" The way is open to them to get help before a problem becomes too serious.

To be sure, availability is more a matter of attitude than schedule. Of course it is necessary for a couple to feel that a pastor really cares about them and their marriage, that he really wants to help, and that he has some ability to help them work out their problem. Then, given this, the expectation of an interview facilitates the acceptance of available help.

Why Six Month?

Why is this fifth session set for one to six months after the wedding? One reason is to leave the date flexible so that the couple can schedule the appointment when they feel it will do them the most good. Enough time must be allowed for them to work on some adjustments on their own, to settle down with each other, as it were. They need to know that help is available, but only if they need it.

The limit of six months is deliberately chosen. These first few months of marriage are crucial.[1] It is the time when two persons who are very different are trying to learn to adjust to each other in the most intimate relationship of life. Generally more differences are evident during this time than at any other period of their marriage. They have less experience in making adjustments and in handling disagreements than at any later time. Consequently, this is the time when they are most likely to need help. They are not yet set in their ways, or resigned to live with their problems without doing something about them. They are still eager to improve their marriage.

These first few months are also the time when the couple is setting patterns of adjustment that are likely to remain with them the rest of their lives. If the proper help is given as needed, they may be able to discover creative and satisfying ways of relating to each other.

Reminders Needed

Experience discloses that only about one in four couples takes advantage of the opportunity for further counseling. This is a significant number which makes the plan worth suggesting to all those who receive premarital counseling.

[1] This is the thesis of Tom McGinnis, *Your First Year of Marriage*, p. 1.

Only about half of the couples in premarital counseling return the books loaned by the pastor without some additional follow-up. Books are usually accompanied by a brief note of appreciation for the counseling and perhaps the message that the newlyweds are doing fine and do not need to see him. The others need to be reminded to return the books. When the pastor writes a reminder letter, he has an excellent opportunity to add a paragraph about the suggested counseling session. He lets them know that they may call him for an appointment at any time. But the decision should be left to them. They should not be made to feel guilty if they do not make an appointment.

With a few couples the pastor takes the initiative in reminding them that he is looking forward to seeing them and suggests that they call him within a certain period of time, perhaps within a few days. However, when they do call, no pressure should be exerted to get them to come in if they do not want counseling at this time. During the conversation the pastor may suggest a book, or indicate that he has one to lend them when he sees them. *Your First Year of Marriage* by Tom McGinnis is a good one for this purpose.

Procedure

How does the pastor conduct the fifth interview? The two approaches of premarital counseling are still appropriate—educative and problem-solving.

Technically, however, the fifth interview is not premarital counseling. It is marriage counseling[2] and should be conducted as such when a couple takes the inititative in seeking counseling and comes with a problem they are ready to work on.

Marital Adjustment Schedule

A very good questionnaire to use here is the Marital Adjustment Schedule 1A.[3] It should be filled out by each of the partners

[2] There are a number of good books in this field, such as Leslie E. Moser, *Counseling: A Modern Emphasis in Religion;* Dean Johnson, *Marriage-Counseling: Theory and Practice;* J. K. Morris, *Marriage Counseling, A Manual for Ministers;* and Charles William Stewart, *The Minister As Marriage Counselor.*

[3] Available from the Marriage Council of Philadelphia, 4025 Chestnut Street, Philadelphia, Pennsylvania 19104.

separately and used by the pastor very much as the Premarital Questionnaires are.

Role Expectancy Inventory

Another resource to guide this interview is A *Marriage Role Expectation Inventory,* by Marie S. Dunn, already referred to. It may be used to encourage communication on any important roles that emerge, very much as suggested in the earlier interview before marriage.

After marriage, a stimulating variation may be used. On his form the husband rates each role according to the way he sees himself *actually performing* the role at the present time. Simultaneously the wife rates another copy of the husband's form according to way she *would like* for him to perform each role. The same procedure is followed in rating two sets of the wife's inventory by both partners. This process allows for the comparison of *role performance* and *role expectation,* which may be a very healthy exercise.

Review the Records

When couples come in primarily to complete the premarital arrangement for the fifth interview, the pastor reviews their premarital counseling records as a part of his own preparation for the session. He may find several concerns or areas which seemed very significant at the time and which he noted for follow-up in the fifth session.

Developmental Tasks

Another approach is to review the couple's developing relationships on the basis of developmental tasks. This is a very comprehensive approach. It is all-inclusive and allows for a rather full examination of the various areas of adjustment, including husband and wife roles. But it does require more skill and much more time than the others suggested.

This approach gives the couple an opportunity to evaluate their success thus far in marriage. It also provides the pastor a framework within which he may structure the content of the interview. He will then adapt any structure or content to the needs of the couple and the time available for counseling.

The developmental-task approach has some distinctive marks. It includes certain areas of adjustment and fits them into a pattern of overall development. Instead of considering one area of adjustment as though it were a separate part of a couple's relationship, as the earlier mentioned subject method is likely to do, the developmental approach emphasizes the interrelatedness of the various tasks.

The tasks are understood as arising from three roots. These are primarily from the total-person maturation (physical, emotional, social, and so forth) of the husband and wife and from the cultural expectations regarding married couples; and, secondarily, from the values and goals of the couple. The developmental tasks are seen as "inner" responsibilities of the couple—no one else can accomplish these for them—and also as foundations for later development. This approach views marriage as a comprehensive, developmental, dynamic growth process, not as a once-for-all achievement.

For a comprehensive coverage, ten developmental tasks should be explored with each couple. The pastor will not try to impose his interpretation of these tasks on the couple but he will, as a minister of the gospel, take the responsibility for helping them see the value of the Christian faith in each task they face. These are the ten developmental tasks.[4]

Developing and Sustaining a Christian Style of Life

This task includes working out a common philosophy of life, a moral and spiritual value system, and personal motivation for living. It also involves agreeing on religious practices in the home and participation in the life and work of the church. Such religious commitment calls for the intermeshing of two formerly differing ways of life, and may be very difficult for some. This is especially true if a husband and wife come from different religious back-

[4] Adapted from Evelyn Millis Duvall, *Family Development.* See Chapter 2 for a description of tasks and Chapter 6 for "Beginning Families: Establishment Phase." Dr. Duvall lists nine tasks. Ten are listed here to call attention to community relationships.

grounds, or if one has been accustomed to being more active in church than the other. One may have no religious inclination at all.

Establishing a common religious philosophy and practice is perhaps both the most difficult and the most important task a couple has. They need to know that this task may take a long time and they may never fully achieve their goal. For life is ever changing and faith is ever growing. They also need to know that this task is worth working at. For it is the foundation of their life together, and it determines the way they work at all the other developmental tasks.

Providing the Necessities of Life

The emphasis here is usually on finding and maintaining a place to live. This may be a small one-room rented apartment or a large fully furnished house. But a couple's task will be to make it home for them. Finding and furnishing the new residence demands many immediate decisions on a joint basis, so different from the previous decision-making. Compromise is often necessary—perhaps in location and in taste in furnishings. One or both of the partners may have to be satisfied with less than they were accustomed to in their parental home.

The necessities of life also include such items as food, clothing, medical care, and transportation. Providing these, too, will call for many joint decisions and adjustments, even though some individual tastes may be respected. The main thing is for the couple to actually experience working together as a team in handling these choices and in getting settled in a home base together. A pastor can help couples not only to be considerate of each other in making their decisions, but also to evaluate their decisions in the light of their values and goals in life.

Earning and Spending Income

The couple must develop mutually acceptable methods of earning and spending their money, and ways of managing and using any possessions or other resources they may have. Marriage may necessitate a change in jobs for one or both persons.

A major item for consideration here is whether or not the wife will work—which is more and more the rule these days. When both husband and wife work it may be necessary to make adjustments in schedules, transportation, and household tasks. The feelings and meanings of these adjustments should be considered.

Again, values and goals play a vital role in spending as well as in earning money. These values and goals should guide the couple in deciding just what amounts they allow in their budget for each item. A budget, or some form of spending plan, should be mutually agreed upon. Decisions must now be made together rather than independently. Marriage also requires more thought for the future, perhaps in the form of savings and insurance. The important question here is this: Does the couple become a unit in arriving at a mutually satisfying earning and spending plan?

Establishing Husband and Wife Roles

Couples must agree on who does what and who is responsible to whom. Today couples have more freedom in managing their affairs. In the past husband and wife roles were more clearly defined. The husband was to be the head of the house, the one in authority. The wife stayed at home and carried the household responsibilities, while the husband went out and worked at his job. With the present-day emphasis on equality between the sexes, and with so many wives working outside the home, the old, clear-cut patterns are changing.

For many couples these changing patterns are creating confusion, and even conflict. Their *feelings* about the changing roles is perhaps more important than what they actually do. A husband may feel he has failed as a breadwinner if his wife works, especially if he grew up in a home where his mother never worked outside the home and his parents placed a high value on the husband's role of supporting the family. Frequently negative feelings, especially a husband's feelings of inadequacy, are not brought out into the open.

Decisions regarding roles should be made by couples together, taking into account their feelings, and considering the wisdom of changing. Otherwise, decisions may be made by default and create an underlying tension. Couples may need help in learning to be sensitive to each other's personal preferences and abilities as they work out their responsibilities together.

Creating and Maintaining Communication

Couples must find meaningful ways of communicating with each other emotionally and intellectually. This means creating a system of two-way give and take, not one partner simply telling the other something.

Learning to be sensitive to each other's feelings is far more important than just hearing the words that are said. Meaning is most likely to be in the feelings. This deeper meaning may also be communicated in actions more than in words. Not that words are unimportant, however, for some words carry a great deal of freight.

Each partner needs to learn not only how to "get the message," but also how to be willing and able to make an appropriate response. In fact, the best kind of communication is that which occurs when one partner is so sensitive to the other's need that he responds before the other is aware of having asked.

Establishing lines of communication also means finding ways of handling disagreements or conflicts. Some couples think they are protecting their relationship by overlooking differences. Just the opposite may be true. Instead of protecting their relationship, they may be making it more superficial and perhaps more fragile. Facing differences and working them through on a problem-solving basis actually strengthens the relationship in most cases.

Couples may need further help from their pastor in learning how to make decisions together, or how to reopen lines of communication once they have been disrupted.

Meeting Personal and Affectional Needs

One of the most important developmental tasks in the beginning of marriage is the couple's establishing mutually satisfying ways of meeting their personal and affectional needs.

By personal needs is meant here the whole area of an individual's psychological or emotional needs which require attention and nourishment from his partner. For example, he may need to be affirmed as a separate individual, as a person of worth, and may need to have his sense of self-esteem fed and strengthened in healthful ways. His need for respect and privacy is part of this total need.

By affectional needs we mean the couple's need for sharing, for mutual give and take, and for fellowship and companionship. One part of this is their need for finding fulfillment with each other in their sexual relations, though not in this area alone.

Couples may need help in understanding that neither the personal nor the affectional needs should be minimized, for both are essential. This calls for a sensitive appreciation of the sometimes ambivalent needs for intimacy and distance, for companionship and privacy, for a sense of belonging and sturdy individuality. And all of these needs are so intertwined that they can be separated only for purposes of examination and evaluation. These needs should be seen as related to interests and activities, some shared and some private, as well as to the whole matter of personality adjustment, already discussed above.

Planning for Children

Another task for couples to face is the possibility of having children and to agree on plans for their coming. This means talking over how many children they would like to have, how soon, and how far apart. Timing is necessarily related to the wife's working.

Today as a total group, more and more couples are having their children earlier after marriage (eighteen months to two years) and closer together in age (about two years). However, a few couples (especially if the wife wants to work for a while or a couple wants to travel, and so forth) are delaying having their first child for several years. Most couples find it best to give themselves enough time to get adjusted to each other before they take on the responsibility of adjusting to a child.

Our church believes that every child should be wanted and planned for as a gift from God. Thus it approves of planned parenthood, and urges couples to get the medical advice available and find the method best suited to their needs. An unplanned pregnancy can be a real crisis in the life of a couple, especially if they are still struggling to get started in life together. But if such a pregnancy does occur, they should know that their pastor is available to help them adjust to the new situation in the most constructive manner possible.

Adjusting to Relatives

The task of adjusting as a married couple to relatives in the larger families of in-laws on both sides is a large one. The adjustment, however, usually centers around getting along with parents.

Many couples feel that only the man and the wife are getting married and that they do not need to concern themselves with their immediate families, and especially not with more distant relatives. But actually two whole families are coming into a new relationship through the marriage. The exact kind of relationship depends on just how close various family members are.

Some couples may have a struggle in establishing their independence from parents. They may need emotional support from their pastor in maintaining the primacy of their own marriage as a new unit and being able to stand on their own feet. One or both persons may still be too dependent on the parents, or may feel guilty about moving out of the parental home, especially when some emotional or financial need is involved. But the separation is necessary if the new marriage is to have life of its own. This does not mean that couples must cut themselves off from their parental families. But it does mean that they will have to find new ways of relating to relatives that will be satisfying.

Making and Keeping Friends

Newly married couples are faced with the task of making many adjustments with friends and associates. The pastor can help them to be realistic in this task at four points.

First, some couples are unrealistic in thinking that they do not need any friends after they are married. They are so much in love with each other and are finding all their interests so absorbing that they think *they* are all they need! Obviously, thinking that two people can meet all of each other's fellowship needs is expecting too much of them and of their marriage. It is all right for the couple to be alone for a time, but soon after the honeymoon they need to move out into social activities with others.

A second mistake some couples make is in thinking that friendships take care of themselves, that they need to do nothing to initiate or maintain friendships. Possibly many social activities involving friends did develop easily and naturally before marriage. But afterward more deliberate effort seems to be required. It may be, too, that popular persons were on the receiving end of friendship before marriage; the girl may have been especially sought out. But marriage changes all this, for marriage has moved the couple into a different world, where responsibilities for entertaining are more equalized.

Third, a couple must decide which of their old friends they want to keep. Most couples come to marriage with three sets of friends—his, hers, and theirs. Each of the partners probably had some friends not very well known to the other. The wife had her girl friends, and husband his boy friends. These friendships may create some tensions after marriage. One person may not like certain of the other's friends, but may not say much about it until after marriage. Maintaining friendships with members of the opposite sex, especially if they are still single, may also raise questions. Often a single person, male or female, is considered a threat by one's partner. It is well for both husband and wife to realize this and find some agreeable way of making decisions and maintaining the relationships both of them want to keep.

Fourth, there is the matter of making new friends. A couple needs to realize the value of new friends, and may need help in actually making contacts. Perhaps the new friends will also be newly married couples, but some may be of a different age group. In either case, friendships may be formed around interests and activities that the couples enjoy or in which they find meaning. The pastor may be able to help the new couple become related to a group in the church or community. Or if they are moving to a new community—as four out of five people do at the time of marriage, or within a year after marriage—he may be able to help them make contact with a congenial group by writing the pastor of the church where they are going.

In addition, couples may find it necessary to adjust to certain business entertaining that is expected of them because of their jobs. Finding a workable plan for creating and sustaining friendships with business associates is also part of this ninth developmental task.

Taking Part in Community Life

The final developmental task of newly marrieds, and one which is often overlooked, is finding a place for themselves in various community activities, orgainzations, or movements. These include state, national, and world interests, even though the focus is often on the local community where they live.

Many young couples are unrealistic in thinking that they can withdraw from the world, and live in isolation from the social forces around them. They need help from their pastor in realizing that they are a part of their community and that they have an opportunity and responsibility to contribute to the shaping of the culture. Social forces impinge on their lives whether they choose to let this happen or not.

Many young adults today have a very keen sense of social responsibility. But they may need help in making their influence effective. They may be very much opposed to many of the things happening in their community, nation, and world; but they may not be as certain about how they can work toward betterment. Some of these young people become disillusioned very quickly, partly because of the hypocrisy and often outright dishonesty they discover among organizations or people whom they have formerly respected, partly because they are unrealistic in expecting reforms overnight. They need our encouragement and support—encouragement to take part in various organizations and movements that are at work for community betterment of one kind or another. They will surely need the pastor's support (and the support of whatever segments of the Christian community can be rallied) if they are not to be discouraged by the opposition they are certain to encounter.

Many young couples may really want to move into various community organizations and activities, but they do not know how to make the necessary contacts. This is more likely to be true if they are newcomers to the community, especially in larger urban areas.

The pastor can guide them to the proper contacts through various other members of the church—one advantage of counseling in the context of the Christian community.

These young couples need the help of their pastor and other members of the Christian community. Joint participation in those aspects of community life on which both agree strengthens their relationship, and their lives and influence can contribute much to the community.

Primarily, however, this developmental task, like all others, is the responsibility of the couple. The pastor, in counseling, can alert them to the task and can stimulate them to work on it. He can encourage them in it, but the task is theirs.

The fifth interview may be a health checkup which reveals everything is in good order. On the other hand, this review may reveal problem areas which require one or more additional sessions for extended counseling. The hope is that whatever approach the pastor chooses will be helpful in solving problems and enriching marriage.

Bibliography

Baruch, Dorothy, and Miller, Hyman. *Sex in Marriage.* New York: Harper & Row, 1962.

Belting, Natalia, and Hine, James R. *Your Wedding Workbook.* Danville, Ill.: Interstate Printers and Publishers, 1963.

Blood, Robert O., Jr. *Marriage.* New York: The Free Press, 1969.

Bowman, Henry A. *Marriage for Moderns.* New York: McGraw-Hill, Fifth Edition, 1965.

Butterfield, Oliver M. *Sexual Harmony in Marriage.* New York: Emerson Books, 1967.

Calderone, Mary S. *Manual of Contraceptive Practice.* Baltimore: Williams & Wilkins, 1963.

Carrington, W. L. *The Healing of Marriage.* New York: Channel Press, 1961 (out of print).

Christensen, H. T., ed. *Handbook of Marriage and the Family.* Chicago: Rand McNally & Co., 1964.

Clinebell, Howard J., Jr. *Basic Types of Pastoral Counseling.* Nashville: Abingdon Press, 1966.

————. *Mental Health Through Christian Community.* Nashville: Abingdon Press, 1965.

Cryer, Newman S., and Vayhinger, John M. *Casebook in Premarital Counseling*. Nashville: Abingdon Press, 1962 (out of print).

Duvall, Evelyn M. and Sylvanus M., eds., *Sex Ways—In Fact and Faith*. New York: Association Press, 1961.

Duvall, Evelyn Millis. *Family Development*. Philadelphia J. P. Lippincott, Third Edition, 1967.

————, and Hill, Reuben. *Being Married*. New York: Association Press, 1960.

————. *When You Marry*. New York: Association Press, 1962.

Eichenlaub, John E. *The Marriage Art*. New York: Dell Publishing Co., 1961.

Erikson, Erik H. *Childhood and Society*. New York: W. W. Norton, Second Edition, 1964.

Fisher, Esther O. *Help for Today's Troubled Marriages*. New York: Hawthorn Books, 1968.

Gordon, Albert I. *Intermarriage: Interfaith-Interracial-Interethnic*. Boston: Beacon Press, 1964.

Greenblatt, Bernard R. *A Doctor's Marital Guide for Patients*. Chicago: Budlong Press, 1968.

Greene, Bernard L., ed. *The Psychotherapies of Marital Disharmony*. New York: The Free Press, 1965.

Gurin, Gerald, and others. *Americans View Their Mental Health*. New York: Basic Books, 1960 (out of print).

Hiltner, Seward. *Pastoral Counseling*. Nashville: Abingdon Press, 1952.

————, and Colston, Lowell G. *The Context of Pastoral Counseling*. Nashville: Abingdon Press, 1961.

Johnson, Dean. *Marriage Counseling: Theory and Practice*. Englewood Cliffs, N. J.: Prentice-Hall, 1961.

Johnson, Paul. *Psychology of Pastoral Care*. Nashville: Abingdon Press, 1953.

Klemer, Richard H. *Counseling in Marital and Sexual Problems*. Baltimore: Williams & Wilkins, 1965.

Landis, Judson T. and Mary G. *Building a Successful Marriage*. Englewood Cliffs, N.J.: Prentice-Hall, Fifth Edition, 1968.

Landis, Paul H. *Making the Most of Marriage*. New York: Appleton-Century-Crofts. Third Edition, 1965.

Mace, David R. *Whom God Hath Joined*. Philadelphia: Westminster Press, 1953.

————. *Success in Marriage*. Nashville: Abingdon Press, 1958.

McGinnis, Tom. *Your First Year of Marriage*. Garden City, N. Y.: Doubleday & Co., 1967.

McHugh, Gelolo. *Marriage Counselor's Manual and Teacher's Handbook*. Durham, N. C.: Family Life Publications, 1968.

Morris, J. K. *Marriage Counseling, a Manual for Ministers*. Englewood Cliffs, N.J.: Prentice-Hall, 1965.

Moser, Leslie E. *Counseling: A Modern Emphasis in Religion*. Englewood Cliffs, N. J.: Prentice-Hall, 1962.

Nash, Ethel M.; Jessner, Lucie; and Abse, Wilfred, eds. *Marriage Counseling in Medical Practice*. Chapel Hill: University of North Carolina Press, 1964.

Oglesby, William D. *Referral in Pastoral Counseling* Englewood Cliffs, N. J.: Prentice-Hall, 1968.

Pearce, Elizabeth C., and Rodgers, Betty S. *Altar Bound*. Danville, Ill.: Interstate Printers and Publishers, 1966.

Peterson, James A. *Married Love in the Middle Years*. New York: Association Press, 1968.

Pike, James A. *If You Marry Outside Your Faith*. New York: Harper & Row, 1962.

Rogers, Carl. *On Becoming a Person*. Boston: Houghton-Mifflin, 1961.

Rutledge, Aaron L. *Pre-marital Counseling*. Cambridge. Schenkman Publishing Co., 1966.

Simon, Paul and Jeanne. *Protestant-Catholic Marriages Can Succeed*. New York: Association Press, 1967.

Smith, Leon, and Staples, Edward D. *Family Ministry—Through the Church*. Nashville: General Board of Education of The United Methodist Church, 1967.

Stewart, Charles William. *The Minister as Marriage Counselor*. Nashville: Abingdon Press, 1961.

Stone, Abraham and Levine, Lena. *The Premarital Consultation, a Manual for Physicians*. New York: Grune & Stratton, 1956.

Terkelsen, Helen E. *Counseling the Unwed Mother*. Englewood Cliffs. N.J.: Prentice-Hall, 1964.

Tournier, Paul. *To Understand Each Other*. Richmond: John Knox Press, 1967.

Trainer, Joseph B. *The Physiologic Foundations for Marriage Counseling*. St. Louis: C. V. Mosby Co., 1965.

Winch, Robert Francis. *Mate Selection.* New York: Harper & Brothers, 1958 (out of print).

Winter, Gibson. *Love and Conflict: New Patterns in Family Life.* New York: Doubleday & Co., 1958.

Young, Leontine. *Out of Wedlock: A Study of the Problems of the Unmarried Mother and Her Child.* New York: McGraw-Hill, 1954.